Return Love to *"Love"*

Return Love to *"Love"*

Compiled by:
Harriet Hammons

PUBLISHING COMPANY
P.O. Box 220 • Goleta, CA 93116
(800) 647-9882 • (805) 692-0043 • Fax: (805) 967-5843

Dedication

This meditation book is for all who are seeking a closer union with our Triune God and with our Blessed Mother, Mary, Ever-Virgin Mother of Jesus. It is dedicated to the Love and Mercy of the Most Holy Trinity, in praise and thanksgiving for all that our God does in our daily walk with Him, surrendering to Him all honor and glory, now and forever.

Library of Congress # 99-75896

Published by:
  Queenship Publishing
  P.O. Box 220
  Goleta, CA 93116
  (800) 647-9882 • (805) 692-0043 • Fax: (805) 967-5843

Printed in the United States of America

ISBN: 1-57918-120-1

Declarations

Since the abolition of Canons 1399 and 2318 of the former Code of Canon Law by Pope Paul VI on October 14, 1966, in the Decree of the Congregation for the Propagation of the Faith, A.A.S., 58, page 1186, publications about new apparitions, revelations, prophesies or miracles, etc., have been allowed to be distributed and read by the faithful without the express permission of the Church and without a Nihil Obstat and Imprimatur.

In Chapter II, No. 12 of the Second Vatican Council's "*Lumen Gentium*" we read:

"The Holy Spirit ... distributes special gifts among the faithful of every rank ... Such gifts of grace, whether they are of special enlightenment or whether they are spread more simply and generally, must be accepted with gratefulness and consolation, as they are specially suited to, and useful for, the needs of the Church ... Judgements as to their genuineness and their correct use lies with those who lead the Church and those whose special task is not indeed to extinguish the spirit, but to examine everything and keep that which is good." (Confer — 1 Thess. 5:19-21)

"Extinguish not the spirit. Despise not prophecies But prove all things; hold fast that which is good. (1 Thess. 5:19-21)

"In cases which concern private revelations, it is better to believe than not to believe, for, if you believe, and it is proven true, you will be happy that you have believed, because our Holy Mother asked it. If you believe, and it should be proven false, you will receive all blessings as if it had been true, because you believed it to be true." (His Holiness, Pope Urban VIII, 1623-44)

It is hereby stated that the messages contained in this book must be understood not as words spoken directly by Our Lord and Our Blessed Mother, but received in the form of interior locutions. These locutions were originally received by Carol Ameche and Harriet Hammons, as directed by Jesus and Mary, to be put into book form as teachings and lessons, and to be called "Do Whatever Love Requires." Harriet Hammons has now been directed to put into a book form meditations for each day of the week and month of the year, by Jesus, based on the teachings and lessons from the book and supplement to the book, "Do Whatever Love Requires." In accordance with the regulations of the Second Vatican Council, the publisher and author states that we do not wish to precede the judgment of the Roman Catholic Church in this matter, to which we humbly submit.

Contents

Declarations v

Preface ix

Introduction by Jesus xiii

JANUARY   Importance of Prayer 1

FEBRUARY   Forgiveness and Reconciliation 19

MARCH   A Cup of Blessing
                — Suffering and the Cross 35

APRIL   Eucharist/Mercy and Love 53

MAY   Mother of God and Our Mother
                — Total Consecration 71

JUNE   The Most Holy Trinity Focus: God
                the Son 89

JULY   The Most Holy Trinity Focus: God
                the Holy Spirit — Defend the Faith 107

AUGUST   The Most Holy Trinity Focus:
                God, The Father 125

SEPTEMBER Trust — Faith — The Will of God 143

OCTOBER   Holiness and Virtues 161

NOVEMBER   Being Prepared — Holy Souls
                — Thanksgiving 183

DECEMBER   New Beginnings — Thoughts to Ponder . . . 203

Prayer Suggestions 223

Thoughts to Reflect on 235

Preface

"Love is patient; love is kind. Love is not jealous, it does not put on airs, it is not snobbish. Love is never rude, it is not self-seeking, it is not prone to anger neither does it brood over injuries. Love does not rejoice in what is wrong but rejoices with the truth. There is no limit to love's forbearance, to its trust, its hope its power to endure . . . There are in the end three things that last . . . FAITH, HOPE, AND LOVE, AND THE GREATEST OF THESE IS . . . LOVE!"
(1 Corinthians 13: 4-7,13)

Nothing is more important than living in total union with our Triune God and with our Blessed Mother. You do this as you get to know Them on a personal level. When you develop this personal relationship with Jesus and Mary, the result will be an ever increasing faith and trust, which will grow more every day in Their love and in Their Hearts. You will find yourself becoming a person of joy and hope, a person of love and understanding, a person of peace and patience. You will soon acquire all the virtues from the Nature of Jesus, which He shares with us and through His complete union with Mary.

We have been asked to bring these words of Theirs to you, on a daily basis, so you can learn to know Them on this personal level which They want. Jesus said, those who choose to use this meditation book of Theirs, this holy tool blest by Them, will find it to be a useful aid in their daily walk with Him as well as giving spiritual direction for their every day living. It will give much hope and consolation to those in need.

As you read these meditations of Theirs, you will find Jesus, the Pearl of Great Price, and Mary, the Morning Star, the most perfect of God's creatures.

Here you will find refuge in Their Two Hearts.

Here you will find home.

Here will be reason and sanity, purpose and the end to illusion.

Here is to be found the fullness of reality and integrity.

Here is the protection and power and strength, fidelity and obedience and truth and answers, which you may be looking for.

Here you will find Someone who is for you, Who is calling to you, encouraging you, helping you, interceding for you, waiting for you, guiding and directing you. This Someone's agenda includes only eternal life and happiness and love for you!

This book contains the teachings from Jesus and Mary, some of the Saints, as well as some from God the Father and God the Holy Spirit. These were taken from Their book, "Do Whatever Love Requires" as well as its supplement, authored by Jesus and Mary and put together by Carol Ameche and Harriet Hammons. Included in this are recent lessons which were deemed important to print as well in these pages for your meditation.

It is recommended, if you wish to go further in depth on any of the meditations found in this book, that you refer to the original book, *Do Whatever Love Requires*, and its supplement. In these two volumes you will find the entire lesson which was given to the hearts of Carol Ameche and Harriet Hammons for your direct spiritual benefit.

Your first guideline to live and to learn holiness is Holy Scripture. Contained in Scripture is a framework for understanding and responding in a progressively deeper way to the Love of Jesus and Mary, the Father and the Holy Spirit. Scripture actually opens our hearts to allow Jesus to work in us to expel our anxieties and frustrations. This way, we learn to perceive His truths with our hearts. Therefore, always give praise and thanksgiving for our good fortune to have His Holy Word.

May the Spirit of God always enlighten and strengthen each of you to persevere in all your resolutions, that you may come "….to know the love of Christ that surpasses all knowledge, so that you may be filled with the fullness of God." (Ephesians 3:19)

St. Teresa, "The Little Flower," had this to say: "You must build your spiritual life out of nothing. To have nothing allows you the opportunity to have it all. To do without, to slow down and pray, to see yourselves as dependent on the Mighty Hand of the Father, will bring each of you to the realization of His great love and devotion to His people. Offer whatever you have in order to perfect your soul and to be of help to others and to serve their needs."

These meditations are about LOVE. They are about returning love for love, TO LOVE. Our Blessed Mother has said that to love is all. The very act by which you were created by Love Itself calls you to love as you are loved. The very Love, which sustains and nourishes you, calls you to sustain and love everyone you meet, with the same fairness and equality and acceptance that you have experienced from God. That same gift of love is free. It is free to be enjoyed and developed and passed along to fill the world with beauty and carefree laughter and peace and safety.

Jesus said to a soul that we should "Love one another because love is of God and everyone who loves is begotten of God, and has knowledge of God ..." He meant that love is not to be kept to oneself. Love is a gift to be shared with others, and in giving our love to others, we give it back to Him. Jesus said, when a gift (love) is kept, it then becomes a possession. This leads to selfishness, self-centeredness, pride and all the darkness the world would have you immerse in. Man's selfish love thus becomes a commodity.

> Where there is love, the heart is light,
> Where there is love, the day is bright,
> Where there is love, there is a song
> to help when things are going wrong...
> Where there is love, there is quiet peace,
> A tranquil heart where turmoils cease.
>
> Oh, blest are you, who walk in love,
> You also walk with God above...
> And when man walks with God again,
> There shall be Peace on earth for men.

THE PATH YOU WALK WITH OTHERS, IN LOVE,
IS THE PATH GOD WALKS WITH YOU!

Introduction

"For I am the Lord, your God, the Holy One of Israel, your Savior. Fear not, for I am with you. You are My witnesses, says the Lord, My servants whom I have chosen to know and believe in Me and understand that it is I, the Lord; there is no Savior but Me." (Isaiah 43: 5, 10-11)

The following introduction to this meditation book, *Return Love TO LOVE,* is given to us by Jesus Himself, through His vehicle, Harriet Hammons. We urge you to continue to read further to see what He is saying to us.

Jesus said: *"Dear ones of My Most Sacred and Merciful Heart, this book you now hold in your hands is one which I have placed there for you to have; just for you! The intention to do this has been in My Heart for you for a very long time now. It was My desire you have it at just the right time in your life when its meaning for you, for your hearts, for your lives, would be accepted by you. As you begin to meditate on the words in this book on a daily basis for the year, you will find Me, the Word, in these words, as well as finding Me in Holy Scripture. I suggest you read the Word every day, My loved* ones, because it will dispel many doubts which you may have. You will find Me in Scripture as you do now in the words you will be reading here each day. You will find the Most Holy Trinity. You will find LOVE!

"There are many things I want you to learn of Me and from Me, but especially one that is close to My Heart. I speak to you about LOVE. You are to find Love through Me, through My Holy Mother, Mary, through My Holy Catholic Church and her teachings as handed down to you from the Apostles, from the holy words in Scripture, from each other and from following all I ask of you. What I ask from you is a great deal, that is, to return love for Love **to** Love (to Me, your God, to the Holy Trinity).

"I would suggest as you meditate on the words found in this little book as well as the words found in Our first book to you, *Do Whatever Love Requires*, that you pray before each meditation, each day, to the Holy Spirit to open your mind and your heart so you can see with your heart, with My Heart, what it is We wish you to know that day through Our words in front of you.

"There is much, dear children, you will get from your deciding to walk with Me through this book to holiness. Keep your heart open to receive all the graces and blessings I wish to give just to you and for you, for that day! Yes, each of you will be blessed individually as you read these words each day. I have blessed this book personally with many graces from its inception. Therefore, as you read the words in these pages, you will know these words are just for you alone, as you continue on this spiritual journey with Us.

"When your openness increases to the words found in these pages, and to Us, and to what We want to do in you and with *you, your spiritual maturity will increase as well. You will then be able to discern and to see and know what it is We have had just for you from the beginning of time.*

"It is My sincerest Heart's desire, dear ones, that you pray to be set on fire with love for Me, for the Most Holy Trinity and that My Real Presence in the Eucharist will come alive for you and in you each time you receive Me in Holy Communion. Pray that My Presence in you and before you will always set you on fire with a deep, burning desire for Love; a Love which you will not understand or be able to comprehend. When you come to that plateau, loved ones, you will know you are truly one with Me and I with you, and that you are truly tasting Heaven within your souls and will know how it will be for you in eternity. In some small way this experience will give you that fire to want Me more and more; then the joy, happiness and peace you experience will be greater than you can imagine.

"I pray, too, that you pray with Me that all My children of all Christian faiths who are in My Body will also become One with Me in this coming together and being completely united with each other and with Me under one Shepherd as I had always intended since that first Eucharistic Banquet. This is My hope and prayer, and is what I wish you to make as your prayer as well, in union with Me.

"When all My children are again One with Me and in Me, then and only then will there, can there be, a true and lasting Peace. Only then will Love live in hearts, beating as one and at the same time with Mine. All My people will then know that I am Mercy, that I am Love, and this is what I want you, all of My children, to know and to live, as I show you.

*"My children, no matter **what** faith you profess, you who believe in Me, in My Father, in Our Holy Spirit, **must** be*

united with Us and with each other through the Immaculate Heart of Our Mary, My Virgin Mother, your mother. I gave her to you from My Cross. She accepted all of you as her children and continues to do so to this very day. She cares for each of you most tenderly. Will you now accept this most Precious Gift, this Jewel of Heaven, into your hearts as gift from Us the Most Holy Trinity? When you do this all my children will then experience and usher in the Triumph of the Immaculate Heart of Mary and the Reign of My Most Sacred Heart. All of Earth will then for the first time experience a true Era of Peace, a peace in hearts, in homes, in families, in churches, in villages and towns, in cities, in countries, in the entire world. Is this what you want?

"My beloved mother has this to say to all of you:"

Mary said: *"To love is ALL! The very act by which you were created by Love Itself calls you to love as **you** are loved. The very Love which sustains and nourishes you calls you to sustain and love everyone you meet with the same fairness and equality and acceptance that you have experienced from God. The same gift of Love is free, my dear ones, free to be enjoyed and developed and passed along to fill the world with beauty and carefree laughter and peace and safety."*

Jesus continued: *"Read this and pray as you meditate on Our Words, dear ones. Open your hearts and minds to the working of Our Holy Spirit within each of you. Then say 'YES' to His working and to His inspiration to you and continue to walk the walk I walk.*

"Be Me! Be Christ-like in all you do! Be like Mary, humble and obedient in all you do. Then make your resolve to Return love for Love — TO Love!

"I bless each of you now as you read this and keep you deep within My Merciful and Sacred Heart for all time to come. AMEN – SO BE IT!"

May Christ dwell in your hearts through Faith and may Charity be the root and foundation of your life. Thus, you will be able to grasp fully with all the holy ones the breadth and length and height and depth of Christ's Love and experience this Love which surpasses all knowledge, so that you may attain to the fullness of God Himself.

"To Him whose power now is at work in us can do immeasurably more than we ask or imagine ... to Him be glory in the church and in Christ Jesus through all generations, world without end. Amen." (Ephesians 3: 17-20)

JANUARY

Importance of Prayer

"Rejoice always, never cease praying, render constant thanks, such is God's Will for you in Christ Jesus." (1 Thes. 5:16-18)

Jesus and Mary have said some very profound things for us to aid in our spiritual walk with Them. **Jesus wants us to fly into the New Year with much joy and confidence that our God is doing and will do what He does best for each of us.** It is said prayer is the conversation of the heart, the communication of the Communion of Saints. All those in Heaven call out to all of us on earth. We are to trust the words of Scripture and the power of our prayers and the mercy of our Savior.

Jesus said: "That where there are two or more praying in My Name, there I am. Miracles do happen and prayers are answered. If only you listen to this simple plea, to these little words, all My children would once again, be in peace and walking the path I take. I love you, My children, beyond your expectations. I hold each of you in My Merciful and Sacred Heart, if you allow Me to. I bless each of you now, in love, peace and joy. Praise and bless the Lord, your God, now and always."

He went on further to say: "Please remember, children, that suffering and sacrifice, united with My suffering and sacrifices for you, will add to the value of all prayers you pray. If it is a sacrifice for you to pray additional prayers and if you have done it in joy, trust, humility and obedience, you have added graces to your own soul and to souls you may not know until you come into eternity with Us."

Reflection for the Month

Jesus presents us with a beautiful parable, giving as an example of candles on an altar during Eucharistic Adoration: *"Dearest children, see how some of the candles on My Altar, in My Presence, are burning so much faster than the others. I liken these candles to a soul, to a heart. Some have many fervent intentions of what they will do and then go at it too fast, without stopping or thinking. This is what I would say to all of this: you pray hard, work hard, do everything too quickly and sometimes you do them very well, while in My Presence. But, while in prayer, whether in My Presence in Adoration or by yourselves in My Presence (meaning perhaps at home), all has been done too fast and with no thought and usually not in real prayer. Before you know it, the flames have gone out (your fervor); you have lost your enthusiasm, your drive, your want and need for Me and for prayer.*

Good prayer is likened to the candles that burn slowly, as you then allow yourselves to ponder and reflect on Me, on My Words, on My Will for you. You need to meditate often and then slowly absorb what it is I am asking of you. Do not let the flames go out, but rather flicker gently, as I Will them to do. You need to be in silence with Me, in the silence of your hearts and minds, to ponder, to know and then to live My Will for you. There is no other way to find Me, to find My Will for your lives. What more could you possibly want or need?"

Prayer

Oh my Jesus and my Love, take all that I have and all that I am and possess me to the full extent of Thy good pleasure, since all I have is Thine without reserve. Transform me entirely into Thyself, so that I may no longer be able to separate myself from Thee for a single moment, and that I may no longer act but by the impulse of Thy pure love. (prayer of St. Margaret Mary)

Resolution

Every day I would like the grace to learn to pray as pleases God best, through the inspiration of the Holy Spirit. That I learn how to pray true prayer, which is the longing of my heart, and to remain in your Will, dear Lord, as no longer do I want my will to exist. I will my will be Yours.

Meditations for January

The Importance of Prayer

"Again I tell you, if two of you join your voices on earth to pray for anything whatever, it shall be granted you by My Father in Heaven. Where two or three are gathered, there am I in their midst." (Matthew 18:19-20)

January 1   (Feast — Mary the Mother of God) New Life

(**Jesus speaks**) How many are truly putting on the "new" in yourselves and shedding the "old"? Those would be the parts that weigh you down and keep you away from Me. Will you truly prepare to take on a "New Life" and walk in "My Light" into the coming year with Me? As your old year now becomes part of history, look forward to this new year with excitement of doing My Will, through increasing your prayer lives. As you begin to meditate now through the year, with Me at the center of your beings, bring all to Me, to My Heart, the only place to find what it is you will need for the coming days and months.

January 2   Treasure of Holiness

(**Jesus Speaks**) Do you not realize that all is taken into account, at every moment, when you pray? There are treasures to be had and to discover each day, as you walk with Me in your quest for holiness, which can only be reached through Me, through prayer to and with Me. Do not cease or let up in this quest, in this search for holiness. You are all meant to be great Saints.

January 3   Praying with the Mother of God

(**Mary Speaks**) Oh what joy you will find as you discover the many merits you will find as you and I continue to walk together. You will journey with me as I take you to Jesus, to the Holy Spirit. At times it may be a rough road with Us, but it is a sure way that leads to heaven, to God the Father of all. Come to me. I will never leave or abandon you to your own wiles. I am your mother and your queen. I am always here for you. Pray with me. Pray to me. Consecrate yourselves and your families to My Jesus, through My Immaculate Heart, then see the miracles that will ensue.

January 4   (Feast — St. Elizabeth Ann Seton)
Two Hearts as One

(**Jesus Speaks**) Remember to consecrate yourselves and your families to Our Sacred Hearts (Mary's Immaculate Heart and My Sacred Heart) every day. When this is done, you are brought into the presence and refuge of two Hearts that are full of love for you and Who will take you into the presence of the Father. Our two Hearts beat as One, breathe as One and act as One. Never leave the perimeter of the protection and safety of Our Hearts. The Consecration to Our Hearts should not be taken lightly and should be done constantly and consistently. This is a sure way to ward off the evils of the world and the flesh. This consecration to

Our Hearts will lead you to a better understanding of My love and mercy.

January 5　(Feast — St. John Neumann, Bishop)
　　　　　All through Mary

(**Jesus Speaks**) Offer all to Me through Mary, My Immaculate Virgin Mother, of your everyday lives, your daily duties, and see what miracles will come. My children, what more can I say but, PLEASE PRAY, PRAY, PRAY WITH US. I love you and am here for you. Call on Me often. Call on the Holy Spirit. Call on your Mother and Queen. Call on your angels and saints. We are all here for you. Listen to this simple plea, won't you? Come walk the path of prayer with Me. **Come to Love.**

January 6　Answered Prayer

(**Jesus Speaks**) Do you, My dear children, realize that all prayer is answered? Do you know how powerful your prayers can be when you, in one heart and voice, give all to Me, and unite them with Me, with Us in Heaven? It is then I take these united prayers, yours and Mine, and plead your cause at the Father's Throne. Do you realize you can change the world by never leaving your homes, your churches, your convents, or your parishes? Yes, your Father in Heaven knows your needs and those you pray for; He knows your hearts.

January 7　To The Father's Heart

(**Mary Speaks**) With prayer, fasting and sacrifices, in union with me and with Jesus, you have the strongest chain to reach to the Father's Heart. I would liken it to my Rosary of prayers. This is one of the strongest and most convincing vehicles you can use before the Throne of Our Just God, all offered with Us (with my Jesus and myself) and through Us, for Our world, for the salvation of souls. Therefore, praise and thank the Triune Godhead at all times for everything and anything, even when it seems impossible to praise and thank Them. This is when your praise, your prayers, your thankfulness, will be accepted with much love and mercy and all will feel that love and mercy shown to them and to the world.

January 8   Continuous Prayer

(**Jesus Speaks**) Dear ones, when you sleep, or think you no longer can add one more prayer, ask your angels and saints and My mother to step in to pray with you and for you. This is then continuous prayer. All you do in everyday daily duties, in My Will, united with Us, is continuous prayer. This will defeat Satan and his cohorts. Pray standing, sitting, lying down, on your knees, but PRAY! Through continuous prayer, your spiritual, as well as physical strength and courage, will be re-enforced each day.

January 9   Your Heart in Your Hand

(**Mary Speaks**) My dearest children, when you pray, pray coming before Jesus with your hearts in your hands, outstretched and giving all to Him, for Him to touch, to heal, to kiss, to love as He enfolds you in the gentleness of His embrace. When this is done, through me, through my heart and hands, I caress your hearts with gentleness and love, kissing each one, thereby opening it wide to my love. This enables me to offer your heart to your God, the Father, and to my Son, Jesus, your Savior, from Whom all things come and from Whom all things evolve.

January 10   Prayer For Conversion And Peace

(Mary Speaks) Please my children, pray unceasingly for conversion; for yourselves, for each other, for Our priest sons, for peace, not only in the world but in your hearts, where peace starts and takes root. Without peace, without conversion, you will always have chaos and division. So come, come now all you my children, away with me for prayer. Come at any hour when My Jesus or I call. My love and peace I continue to bestow on all who wish to come under the mantle of prayer with me, to My Son, Jesus.

January 11   (Feast — St. Hilary, Bishop/Doctor) Listen

(Jesus Speaks) Little ones, dialogue, talk (pray) with Me and to Me. This means prayer. This IS prayer. Pray, pray and then LISTEN. Listen in the silence of your hearts, as I take you to realms you cannot even conceive, but which are available to you for the asking. I am inviting you to storm Heaven with Me at your side (meaning prayer). I want to show the Father how much love there is on His earth, for Him and for each other, by a unity of prayer on the earth, with the prayer in heaven and with the prayer of those in purgatory, as well. We will, with this effort on all our parts, bring Him bouquets of the finest love and mercy We have at Our command. As you pray with each other and in reparation, not only for your sins, but the sins of all your brothers and sisters, in the Body of Christ, uniting all with Us in Heaven, the response will be overwhelming and will soften the Heart of the Father.

January 12   Balance in Prayer

(**Mary Speaks**) Dear children, much depends on your prayer to and with Us, in order to keep what should be a normal balance in your daily lives and to try to drive away the evil that is invading and permeating everyone today. Do whatever you can to encourage all to pray without ceasing. Practice this in your everyday lives. Pray the Rosary, meditate on all the mysteries every day and pray The Chaplet of Mercy for souls. Take your Consecrations to Jesus through me seriously, consecrating yourselves daily. Pray for Peace. Live the Commandments and the Virtues. **You must live each day as if it were your last.**

January 13   Consecration Prayer

(**Jesus Speaks**) Dear ones, through your total consecration to Me through the Immaculate Heart of Mary and through consistent, continuous prayer, you will begin to see as if you did not see. The eyes of your hearts will be leading you and you will be conducting your hearts to control your thoughts. You will begin to hear as if you did not hear, because then only will you understand what you hear. Even though you still hear what the world is saying and see what it is telling you, the eyes of your heart will be set on Me, on the kingdom of God.

January 14   Benefits Of Prayer

(**St. Joseph speaks**) Through prayer, complete trust and faith, with wisdom, became the seat of the holiness we experienced in our little family. We relied on and expected all from our God. Through prayer all things were possible and were in our day-to-day lives. You will find dear children, that this is still so in your lives today. If you only realized the merit and many benefits and knowledge you acquire through prayer, you would never stop. This is especially so with prayer in the family.

January 15   (Feast — Our Lady of Prompt Succor)
Pray While Asleep

(**Mary Speaks**) My precious ones, as you sleep you can ask your angels and saints, as well as those holy souls in purgatory, to continue your prayer from the day. In this way there is never a minute without prayer that will be ascending to my heart and to the Throne of the Most High.

January 16   Family Prayer

(**Mary Speaks**) All families should come to me so I can help them know My Son. Dear ones, come to me with faith and trust. Come to me and accept my love which I hold in My Immaculate Heart, for you and for every family. Prayer leads to peace in families. When you do not pray together or cannot, then each individual must pray for them (others in the family) for the grace to understand the value and importance of this grace, this gift that is communication with their God and Creator. Please children, consecrate your family to the Holy Family, asking this Holy Family to intercede so your family will become holy and one as They are. They are THE FAMILY each family should be patterned after. Children, when you pray as a family, it pleases your Father beyond comprehension. He sees only HIS families, HIS beloved ones, kneeling before Him, in complete adoration of Him, communicating their love for Him, in awe and thanksgiving for what He has done for you. He then blesses each member of this His little family church, in much abundance, with graces untold.

January 17 (Feast — St. Anthony, Abbot)
Family Consecration

(**Jesus Speaks**) Beloved, when you consecrate your families to My Sacred Heart, through Mary's Immaculate Heart, you immediately gain strength, courage and the grace to persevere in the moral and holy standards I continue to set before all of you. This will give your family peace and love. A new prayer life in your families will evolve. I will give you gifts untold and graces you will need. All families who consecrate themselves to Me must renew this family consecration often, together and individually.

January 18 Responsibility

(**Mary Speaks**) Dear children of Mine, when you have consecrated your hearts to Jesus through My Immaculate Heart, your responsibility to Us begins and increases. Jesus and I take all of you: your bodies, your souls, your hearts, your works, all that is interior and exterior, as well as those whom you have consecrated to Us. You are then all Ours and We are all yours. Pray with one heart and mind, in unity with the Holy Spirit and in union with Jesus and myself at all times. With the great gift of giving yourselves to me, through total consecration to Jesus through My Immaculate Heart, you will receive many graces and blessings. This does not mean you will be immune to the working of Satan in your lives. So beware, because Satan hates this consecration. He will intensify his ways of deceit more so now, in your lives. This is not just another devotion, it is a way of life, a way that will lead to your holiness and a way to please the Triune God. (note: see consecration in prayer appendix.)

January 19   Praying for Priests

(**Mary Speaks**) I, your mother, would like you to continue to join me, join all of Heaven in prayer with Jesus, to the Father, for Our loved priests, bishops, religious and Our most beloved Pope. Our priests are the ones who bring Jesus to you through the Consecration at the Holy Mass. You need my priest sons and they need you. Pray with me unceasingly, day and night for them, letting them know you are praying with and for them, that you support them and the truth as handed down from Jesus, through His Vicar on Earth. Nothing is impossible through prayer. Our adversary hates and despises Our priests because they represent Jesus on earth. Be on guard as he will try to dissuade you from praying for them. Bring all to Our Sacred Hearts where refuge is found.

January 20   (Feast — Ss. Fabian & Sebastian) Finding God

(**Jesus Speaks**) My little ones, please remember, the Mass is the primary prayer, with Communion followed by the Holy Rosary. These, when done in the purity of hearts and in the state of grace, can stay events and put a stop to some catastrophes. Adore Me, Praise Me, Thank Me for everything. Let Me know I am God and that I do play an important part in your lives; that I am at the center of your worlds, your very beings. There is no better way to find Me than to be with Me in the silence of your hearts, before Me, in adoration. In this way, you too, can then find My Will for your lives. What more could you possibly want? Am I not sufficient to supply you with everything?

January 21   (Feast — St. Agnes) Prayers of Praise

(**Mary Speaks**) Dear ones, praise to the Father, the Son and the Holy Spirit should always be in your heart and on your lips. Praise and thanksgiving are the sweetest sounds to ascend to the Heavenly Throne. There need be no words to do this, just a lifting of your hearts, minds, and then uniting it with mine, which then is united to Them. Then let your prayer sour as on the wings of a bird, as a dove.

January 22   Praying with your Angels

(**Mary Speaks**) Dear ones, pray night and day. Your guardian angels love to pray with you. Invite them more often. The

Saints in Heaven love to join their prayer with yours. Invite them. All the choirs of Angels pray with you, when asked to join you in prayer. Their songs and prayers are glorious notes taken to the throne of God. It then all becomes one song of praise and thanksgiving at all times. Gloria's. Hosana in the Highest. What joy this gives the Father's Heart.

January 23   Vigil Prayer

(**Mary Speaks**) My children, there are many ways to pray. All night vigils of prayer are most important. Eucharistic Adoration vigils are the best kind of vigils. This appeases the Heart of Jesus and God the Father. I would invite as many as can to hold three-day-and-night vigils of prayer and fasting, preferably in front of the Blessed Sacrament or in your homes, invoking the mercy of the Father on His people through Jesus. I will be praying with you at these times and will send many angels to pray with you. Give these prayers then to Jesus, to Me, as we take them to the Father for you and for the world.

January 24   (Feast — St. Francis de Sales, Bishop/Doctor) Silent Prayer

(**Mary Speaks**) Advance, dear children, in your prayer lives, especially through the silence of heart-to-heart prayer before Him when in adoration of Him. Let Him, His Words absorb your beings and then trust in faith, what He wishes of you and from you. THEN FOLLOW HIM! When you receive Him in Holy Communion, it is then that the silent prayer from your heart of praise, thanksgiving, joy and love touch Him most and fill His Heart with your mercy. He loves it when He and you are united in Communion and are wholly joined in love and mercy. As you spend more time in prayer with Us, in the quiet of your hearts, a new awareness of peace descends upon you. You will then be able to go from one task to another with ease, making of each one a prayer to offer to the Father. Remember, the most important duty is that of prayer and living in the presence of your God.

January 25 (Feast — Conversion of St. Paul) Before Prayer

(**Jesus Speaks**) Dearest children, please ask for the grace of being emptied before you begin to pray. Seek and ask for union with Me every moment of your day. Abandon all of who you are and receive all of Who I Am. Remember too, My little ones, when you have finished each task of your day and before you go on to the next one, please stop and give thanks to the Father for that task and all the He allows you to do for Him and all He is doing in your life. Seek Me and you will find Me.

January 26 (Feast — Ss. Timothy and Titus, Bishops) Simplicity in Prayer

(**St. Theresa of Avila speaks**) Prayer must remain simple. Prayer must be an outpouring of your hearts and thoughts and needs to the Triune Majesty and to the glorious Virgin Mary. Believe in the power of your prayer to help lead you closer to Our Jesus. Prayer is the conversation of hearts, the communication of all the Communion of Saints. **Always trust the words of Scripture, the power of your prayers and the mercy of our Savior.**

January 27 (Feast – St. John Chrysostom) Spiritual Nourishment

(**Jesus Speaks**) My beloved, you need to stand firm on faith, hope and trust. It is in and through prayer, even when you do not feel like praying, that your spiritual strength will build and a wall will be built around you by grace, to be able to ward off the evil that wants to possess you. Do not let anything overshadow My Light. Come to Me to be nourished, to be fed by Me, in the silence of your hearts, joining your hearts with Mine. You need this quiet. Come into the garden of My Heart where you will find the answers you need. I invite you to come each day and join your Fiats (yes), with Mary's, in complete trust and love. You then will see miracles and transformations.

January 28 (Feast – St. Thomas Aquinas) Sacramentals

(**Mary Speaks**) My dear children, the Rosary will be your weapon, as will the Scapular be your shield. Always wear blest objects. Satan hates the Rosary and the Eucharist. He will try to convince you these are not needed. Listen to me, your mother, and always hold the Rosary. Call on Jesus' Name often. Invoke St. Michael and His Angels and your Guardian Angels Then **pray, pray, pray.** Each day continue to consecrate yourselves and everyone to Jesus through me. This is your only hope and this is the sign my Angels will look for; your sign, the sign of my heart, on each of your heads and hearts, will counter the sign of the beast.

January 29   Heavenly Crowns

(**Jesus Speaks**) My people, many gifts are being poured out for Our people. Please pray that all will accept them. Your prayers are the jewels which adorn your heavenly crowns. Prepare yourselves now to approach the throne of My Father in gleaming finery. Dear ones, all prayer is answered, please remember this. Prayer is the key to Our Hearts. I am at this very moment, as you read this, knocking at the door of your heart. Please listen carefully and you will hear My call, My knock.

January 30   Need For Prayer

(**Jesus Speaks**) My beloved ones, do not cease or ever let up on your prayer. I urge you to increase prayer even more, even to the limit that you think you cannot. Your spiritual, as well as physical strength and courage, will need to be re-enforced each day. This can only be done through prayer. The Litany of Humility is recommended to be said daily and should be lived completely. You then die to yourself and become nothing in the eyes of the world and yourselves. Oh what wonders and transformations will then take place. I plead with you to please find the time to unite and pray with Us in Heaven. I then take all to The Father for your world and for souls. I plead continuously before the throne of the Father for all Our children and for your world. (see Litany of Humility in prayer appendix at end.)

January 31   (Feast — St. John Bosco) Pray, Pray, Pray

(Jesus Speaks) Continue, dear ones, to pray My Chaplet of Divine Mercy, My mother's Rosary, as often as you can, for souls, for your world, giving your prayers to Us, to use where We know they are needed most and for whom they are needed at that moment. Praying the Chaplet of Divine Mercy, asking your Angels and Saints to pray with you, enables souls to pass easier from your world to their Eternal reward with Us. I can assure you it has helped many. One day you will know how important this has been, when you see the souls you have helped by these prayers. When you come in Adoration to visit with Me, praying to Me and with Me, all of Heaven is there with you.

FEBRUARY

Forgiveness and Reconciliation

"All this has been done by God, Who has reconciled us to Himself through Christ and has given us the ministry of reconciliation. I mean that God, in Christ, was reconciling the world to Himself, not counting men's transgressions against them, and then He entrusted the message of reconciliation to us." (2 Cor. 5:18-19)

This is a good month to reflect on the Prodigal Son. Put yourself in place of each of the characters: the prodigal son (younger one); the older son; and then the father. How do you see yourself in these three. Perhaps you don't. This is the classic story of forgiveness, reconciliation and coming home.

Jesus has said so many times: "Come to Me each day to pray with Me and to Me, in front of the Blessed Sacrament, so you can be fed spiritual food of which you are in such need. Please try to do this at least for **one hour each day.** Allow Me to heal you by being one with Me. I love you."

Further Jesus says: "Please remember, little ones, that God is always here for you. His tender love, unconditional mercy and forgiveness are offered for each one who comes in humility and seeks to reconcile with the Triune God, Who calls you back to Himself that He might heal you and hold you tenderly, lovingly in His Heart. This is done all through My Sacred Heart and through the Immaculate Heart of Mary. The one who loves and admits he or she is a sinner and asks for Our forgiveness, repents in love, mercy and gratitude, is forgiven."

Jesus also pleads with us: "Dear children, if only you would acknowledge your sins and sinfulness and then come back to Him Who created you, in total trust and obedience, full of humility and love, then there would be harmony and peace, in your hearts, families, country and in the world. Unfortunately, some of you have chosen the dark path to follow, as the world dictates. The world has handed you a tempting piece of cheese and you have and are taking it. Why is this, My children?"

Reflection for the Month

The Father, our God, wants to, He longs to, transform us through the outpouring of much grace upon us. God invites each of us to come to Him through the confessing of our sins. He offers us His Holy Spirit to help us and to give us the necessary power we need, to overcome the darkness in our hearts. God wants to show us our sins so we can come to Him as His little child and cling to Him more fully in absolute trust and love. God can set us free if we allow Him to. He asks, (and this may be difficult) that we turn away from sin and turn back to Him in obedience and trust.

Jesus is offering us the same cup that He offered to His Apostles. This is the same cup that our Savior, Jesus, drank from. It is the cup of suffering and it is also a cup of blessing. As we drink from this cup we will find how we do become true sons and daughters of the Father, His children. He will allow us, through grace, to be able to know the Father intimately, as Jesus does, Himself.

Prayer

My sweet Jesus, I bring my sinfulness before you and ask you to please help me, forgive me so that I may be purified and once more then will be able to walk in your ways. Teach me too, dearest Lord, how to forgive others and myself, as you forgive, and then to forget, knowing that I have been forgiven as well.

Resolution

Every day I will call on the Holy Spirit to convict me of my sins and give me the grace of the Virtues I will need to overcome my faults. I would rather die than sin against my Jesus.

Meditations for February

Forgiveness and Reconciliation

> "For if, when we were God's enemies, we were reconciled to God by the death of His Son, much more, being reconciled, we will be saved by His Life. Not only that; we go so far as to make God our boast through our Lord Jesus Christ, through whom we have now received reconciliation." (Romans 5:10-11)

February 1   Seeing Your Faults

(**Jesus Speaks**) Dearest ones, I cannot penetrate a heart who refuses to acknowledge it could be wrong; one that cannot admit its own sinfulness. There are some of My children who see the sins and faults of others and refuse to see themselves as I see them. Reconcile I beg you, NOW, with Me, with your loved ones, with yourself and get back on the path that leads to Eternal light and happiness. Be humble and obedient of heart and continue to walk in My Light.

February 2   (Feast — Presentation of Lord) Want to Change

(**Jesus Speaks**) Please pray to begin to realize how important it is to get rid of "self." Too many want to **change** others but not themselves. There are those that judge others and the actions of others, but do not take a good, close look at themselves. **The heart is a perfect mirror.** This should mirror

Me, your Lord and Savior. You are hard hearted and stubborn when you refuse to love as I love, as I have asked of you. When you see only the faults of your neighbor and only see how good you are, you have neither charity or mercy, towards yourself, your neighbor or towards Me.

February 3   (Feast — Ss. Blasé & Ansgar)
              Accept Forgiveness

(**Jesus Speaks**) Dear children, rejoice when the Holy Spirit shows you new ways to repent and to obtain graces and forgiveness. Humbly accept your weaknesses and beg My Mercy. It is these very weaknesses that bring each of you to Me. They act as an opportunity for obtaining a deeper love and gratitude that will spring from the depths of your hearts. You who love and admit you are a sinner and ask for forgiveness, repent in love, mercy and gratitude, are forgiven. You are completely forgiven because of Our undying, unconditional love for you. There is no sin too big or too small to be forgiven, if you ask. If you do not ask, you will not receive this forgiveness. You may even doom yourself to eternal darkness instead of Eternal Light.

February 4   Healing of Hearts

(**Mary Speaks**) Beloved children, there must be much reconciliation of hearts. **Please pray for the healing of your hearts.** Pray for the ability to see yourselves now as God sees you. This will purify you and enable you to help others. Pray to St. Michael to protect you from the evil one's deception. Pray with your guardian angels to enlist their help in all you do. PLEASE get on your knees, little ones, begging for His forgiveness. **Reconcile now** and then praise and thank Him for everything. Jesus cannot resist a truly humble and repentant heart, nor will He deny your requests.

February 5   (Feast — St. Agatha) Acknowledge Sinfulness

(**Mary Speaks**) My little ones, the pain in Our Hearts (Jesus' and mine) is unbearable with so much apathy, indifference and turning away from, instead of, to Him. Do not continue in your moral darkness of sin. Please acknowledge the fact of your sinfulness and come to your Lord and God with your hearts in your hands, asking for forgiveness before it may be too late. It would be so easy for you, Our children, to just be Our children, in all humility, trust, faith and obedience. Do not put off repentance. **There is no time to put off coming to God.**

February 6   (Feast — St. Paul Miki & Companions) Conversion

(**St. Anthony speaks**) My brothers and sisters, without a conversion of heart you will never be able to accept anything of what our God wishes for you, for you will be too much imbedded in the world and of the world. You need to be in His Spirit and with His Spirit. This is done by constant, vigilant prayer to Him for this grace to be able to hear His voice and for the grace to WILLINGLY CHANGE the areas of your lives that He will speak to you about. What joy, peace and understanding will fill you when you completely abandon yourselves to **change and to come to Him wholly.**

February 7   Giving All To Mary

(Mary Speaks) Dearest children, take your nothingness, your imperfect person, your sinful souls and give them to me. I will offer them to Him from my hands and from My Immaculate Heart. I take all to Him, including your tears of remorse, of repentance, your asking forgiveness for yourself and the world and your making reparation to Him for the world. He died for all and rose from the dead once and for all time, conquering sin and evil. You must now help in this redemptive act with me. Bring all your imperfections to me as I give them to Him. Then beg for forgiveness.

February 8   (Feast — St. Jerome Emiliani)
Healing Heart

(Jesus Speaks) My sweet ones, much reparation must be made for all the serious and terrible crimes of sin being committed against the Creator and against My Sacred Heart. My own Heart can heal you when our hearts are placed close together. There is no other way to experience peace and gratitude. The cup of My love spills over from My Heart onto yours and bathes you in contentment and a serene love. These are results that last forever. Dear ones, never look back even to yesterday. Once a sin is confessed and is forgiven, it is gone forever.

February 9   Humble Act

(Jesus Speaks) Beloved of My Sacred Heart, it is a humble act to beg. It is a saving act to beg forgiveness for one's sins and to confess them to Me. Praise the Father and thank Him for His gifts and above all, for His Divine Will in your life. Come to Me, My children, and ask Me for forgiveness. Repent and then live as you know love demands. You will then see with the heart of love and mercy. You will want to forgive everyone and anyone that needs your forgiveness. You will want, more than anything, to be forgiven. Oh to be set free! What joy you will have. This is a grace that can be within the reach of each of you.

February 10   (Feast – St. Scholastica) Roots of Sin

(**Mary Speaks**) Dear children, fight with all your might against the wiles of the enemy. He is ever active against those who love and serve me, serve and love Jesus. The important thing is to discover the roots of your personal sin and then bare it to My Son in the Sacrament of Reconciliation. The ability to be humble and obedient will be your greatest assets. Please continue to come to My Son more and more.

February 11   (Feast – Our Lady of Lourdes)
Desire to Repent

(**Bl. Faustina speaks**) Dear brothers and sisters in Christ, when you go to confess your sins, you must have a sincere desire to repent and make up. You must want to reconcile for these sins and then truly be sorry. You should be determined to strive for sanctity always in an effort to reconcile with your Lord. If you are not open and sincere, in all humility, when you come to confess your sins, you put yourself at risk of not benefiting from your confession. A soul must have complete sincerity and openness and it must be humble and obedient.

February 12   Humble Act to Beg

(**Jesus Speaks**) Dearest children, more of you need to know of the rich gifts My Father has for those who come seeking My forgiveness. All My children have the opportunity of being renewed by My Hand, if they would only ask My forgiveness and pledge Me their sorrow and eagerness to repent. This then would be the key to releasing all of the gifts stored up for every person since before their birth. **It is a humble act to beg. It is a saving act to beg forgiveness for one's sins and confess them to Me!** Receive the Sacrament of Reconciliation as though you might not have the opportunity again.

February 13   The Promise

(**Jesus Speaks**) My children, seize the moment and run to Me. Be assured of forgiveness and mercy. This has always been My promise to you. It has never been so important to believe and act on this promise, NOW! Nothing happens unless I allow it and want it for your growth to reconcile, to open eyes and hearts to see your own pride. Then I give each the choice to repent and start over. I pray with all of you that you come to Me to ask for forgiveness and then to forgive each other.

February 14   (Feast — Ss. Cyril & Methodius)
                    Sacrament of Love

(**Jesus Speaks**) Dearest children, **not one soul do I want Lost!** Come to Me in My Sacrament of Love and reconcile with Me, with your neighbor and with yourselves. Come often to My Sacrament of Reconciliation even with the slightest sin, as this is a sure way of grace, of showing Me that you have contrition, repentance and that it is from your heart. Come to Me in all humility, obedience and trust in Me for forgiveness. Do not cling to your sins of pride. Do not refuse to fight these sins of pride. Once a soul has rid itself of all excess baggage, it then can get down to basics … that of LOVE. You need to forgive as I forgive and love as I love. That is why a good, sacramental confession is so important.

February 15   Heavenly Physician

(**Jesus Speaks**) I love you, My children, no matter what you have done. I wish for you to be united to My Sacred Heart, where you will be healed. You must spend much of your time in prayer and remorse for this, with Me, your Physician, much like you would spend time in a hospital being healed of physical wounds. When you come to Me to be healed, be assured you are forgiven. Reconcile with your God, with each other and forgive each other before it is too late. Do this NOW. Spend all the time you need with your Beloved Doctor, Who longs to bind and heal those wounds with His Precious Blood and His Love.

February 16   Die to Self

(**Jesus Speaks**) Loved ones, **self, self, self must die!** You must live your Baptism of purity of heart, mind and soul. When you find yourself being tempted, come to Me, to My Mother, Mary and to My Holy Spirit. Only sin can drive Us away from you. Satan will try to show you the futility of it all. Resist him with all that is in you. Call on Us. We are never away from you.

February 17   Would You Choose Hell?

(**St. Teresa of Avila speaks**) Dear sisters and brothers, what would you do if you were to see hell and all the souls who suffer there? I did. I saw the place in Hell that was saved for me and I was immediately convinced of the need to come back to God. Through the gracious gift of God, I stopped a life of self-deception. I received clarity of mind to accept myself as I really was and the strength and good sense to return at once to all I had professed myself to be.

February 18   Regular Confession

(**Mary Speaks**) Dear ones of My Immaculate Heart, regular confession is so very important because sin, any sin, will hamper the grace that He wants to give each of you. I urge you my children, to keep your souls in the state of grace, in the state of Sanctifying Grace, at all times. In the great Sacrament of Confession you meet Him, where you receive all His love and tender mercy. I caution you to take care of your souls as you take care of your bodies, but even more so.

February 19   (Feast — St. Joseph)
Have You Forsaken Me?

(**Jesus Speaks**) My dearest children, I said from the Cross, "My God, My God, why have You forsaken Me?" Now I say to you, you who are so dear to My Heart, why do you forsake

Me? Why do you continue to turn your backs on Me? Why do you continue to say "no" by delighting in your sins? Why do you continue to follow what the world has to offer? **Why? Why?** Come please, little ones, back to Me now, with all your hearts and souls, your very beings, with your hands outstretched to Me, giving all to Me. Oh how I have waited for your coming back to Me and I will continue to do so until the end of time.

February 20   The Kingdom to Earth

(**Jesus Speaks**) Dearest children, to bring the Kingdom of God to earth, into your very lives, your very beings, you must be able to **FORGIVE** one another as I forgive you. How much pride and judgmentalism have you allowed to be stored in your hearts? How much have you allowed the evil of the world to deceive you into thinking so righteously and judgmentally of your brothers and sisters? Why is it so hard to forgive one another? Why is it so hard to love one another? I invite you to ponder these questions, with Me, in your hearts.

February 21   (Feast — St. Peter Damian, Bishop/Doctor) Our Father…

(**Jesus Speaks**) Children, you say the prayer, Our Father, every day, asking for forgiveness from the Heavenly Father, saying you will forgive, but do you? Do you overlook the faults of others? Without being able to forgive, even the slightest flaw of your brother or sister, you cannot possibly love as I love. You then present Me with a dilemma of not being able to forgive you, when you cannot forgive, as I long to do. Please do not be so hard-hearted and self-centered.

February 22   (Feast – Chair of St. Peter)
                    Forgive Your Brother

(**Jesus Speaks**) Dear ones, reflect on the possibility of going to your brother (sister) and telling him you forgive him and in turn, if need be, ask him to forgive you any transgressions you may have caused him. Words, words, dear children, are like a sword at times. Your words can cut to the heart of your brother or sister in a way that so much irreparable damage is done. **Forgiveness is the key that will set you free. To forgive and be forgiven is likened to being washed clean in the waters of grace.** To forgive could be a means of salvation for your soul and the souls of those who need to hear from you.

February 23   (Feast – St. Polycarp) Lift Veil Of Pride

(**Jesus Speaks**) It is My desire, My children, that you walk the walk I walk in this life to attain holiness. This too will bring the Kingdom of Heaven to earth. You cannot do this while allowing **pride** to cover your hearts, minds and souls with a veil that hides Me from your presence and obstructs Me from entering into your very beings. You then are not allowing Me to be as one with you as it was always meant to be.

February 24   Cause of Pain

(**Jesus Speaks**) My beloved children, why do you cause each other such pain? Do you know when you cause one of

My children pain; you cause Me extreme pain? It is like being crucified all over again on that Cross. My children, what will it take for you to discover forgiveness? Have you not found My merciful forgiveness when you have asked? Have I given My compassion My mercy, My love to you when you asked? Please then, show that same mercy and love to each other whom you need to reconcile with, as I have shown you. Forgive one another, Cherish love. Do all as I do, then you will have love and mercy and you will also then have Me. My peace is yours now and forever, if only you continue to live, love, and walk in My Light. This peace then would be a peace that would be lasting.

February 25   "Old Self"

(**Jesus Speaks**) My children, I ask you to pray for a thorough cleansing of the old and sometimes imagined hurts done to the "old self" so I can work My miracle of healing your hearts. Without this healing of your heart, a changing of "old self" you become self absorbed. It is imperative everyone die to self; kill that old self and this can only be done by you with My grace, through prayer and reconciliation, as it takes your free will to do this. Satan loves to play on self, self-ishness, self-centerdness, anything of "self" that shuts Me out and restricts My Holy Spirit from working within you. Pray for this grace.

February 26   Weakness Because of Sin

(**Jesus Speaks**) Dear children, it would be beneficial for you to wake up to the fact of your sinfulness, your weaknesses because of your sinfulness. Sins of pride and arrogance dull your senses, especially those of morality. Please avoid the "me" attitudes in your lives as well as your sluggish complacency. There is no offense that will not be forgiven if you come in **true** contrition of heart and soul to Us. Come back now to Our loving embrace while the opportunity exists. Hide within My Wounds that you see on the Crucified Christ and there you will find comfort, peace, love and forgiveness. I DIED for you, now if you will it, you will die for Me.

February 27 Working of Holy Spirit

(**Jesus Speaks**) My children, the Holy Spirit is working in many hearts and souls by showing them how We see their souls and giving them the opportunity of repentance to come back now to Us in love. Amend your lives! Change! Be another Me. Come back to the loving arms of the Father, in all obedience and humility, showing your love by your repentance and true contrition of heart, soul and mind. Fight the temptations to sin and to the committing of the same faults again and again. Stand up and fight Satan NOW, under the banner of My Cross and of Reconciliation.

February 28 Ask for Grace

(**Jesus Speaks**) My dear ones, ask Me, ask the Holy Spirit, for the grace to see yourself as your God sees you. Ask to be within the refuge of Mary's Immaculate Heart and close to Joseph, for their help in everything. Ask your guardian angels to stay near you, and help in keeping Satan away. Ask the Holy Spirit to pour into your soul perseverance to be able to overcome all obstacles put in your way of coming back to Us. Ask Our Holy Spirit to enlighten your minds and hearts at all times, especially to the state of your soul and the sins you may have on your soul.

February 29   Forgive is to Love

(**Jesus speaks**) My loved ones, come to Me please NOW dear ones, for the time grows short. You need to love as I love and forgive as I forgive. You must forgive and ask to be forgiven! It is so sad that many have the sin of pride and refuse to fight it. Children, do not give in to the world, but rather listen to that little voice within you which is pleading with you to come to Me, to repent and then come into My Loving Arms and Heart. This is your only sanctuary from all the evil that surrounds you day in and day out.

MARCH

A Cup of Blessing –
Suffering and the Cross

"If a man wishes to come after Me, he must deny his very self, take up his cross, and follow in My steps. Whoever would preserve his life shall lose it; but whosoever shall lose his life for My sake and the gospel, will preserve it. What profit does a man who gains the whole world and destroys himself in the process? What can a man offer in exchange for his life?" (Mark 8:34-37)

It is hard to think of suffering as a "Cup of Blessing." But, that indeed is what it can be and should be to each of us who wish to carry our cross, as He, our Jesus, has asked us to do, and follow Him. When we decide to turn from sin and turn to Him in complete trust and obedience, Jesus then offers us the same cup He offered to His apostles and disciples. It was and still is a "**cup of blessing**." As we drink from this cup (by saying a consistent and constant "yes" to Him) we will know the full benefits of truly being "children of God." We will then know the Father intimately, as Jesus does, and as the Father wishes so much for us. We will see our sin more clearly and how much sin is in opposition to God.

To console the grief-stricken is an act of mercy; for the grief-stricken to console, is an act of sublime charity!

Scripture says that the God of mercies and of all consolation comforts us in all our afflictions and by this enables us to comfort those who are in need of comfort. Because we share in the suffering of Christ, so do we share abundantly in His consolation. This in itself should give us great hope and joy. God knows our situations better than we do. What is more, He can work in situations where, by human standards, all hope is lost. By persevering in prayer, we will learn to release each situation, our situations, into the Hands of God. Doing this, our faith will slowly grow and God's calling for us will unfold.

Reflection for the Month

(by Victorino Osende O.P. from his *Fruits of Contemplation*)

Christian suffering sanctifies all things; And, Divine Love sanctifies all suffering! Suffering, to the human mind, seems irreconcilable with our image of an "all-good and loving" God. Only in the light of the supernatural order do we find the key to the great mystery of suffering.

Through suffering, all things are restored; justice is re-established; man is reconciled with God and reinstated in His friendship, grace is imparted to the soul and sanctification is achieved. Suffering is the great agent of our purification and the eternal guarantee of our humility. Humbled and purified we are restored to the Image and Likeness of God. These marvelous effects of suffering are produced only if the suffering is sent from God and **is accepted with patience.** We must suffer in union with the Spirit of Christ. It doesn't matter if the suffering comes to us as a consequence of our sins and in expiation of them. God never wills sin. But He will use the suffering from sin to draw us to His Sacred Heart, keep us humble and as a most efficacious means for our sanctification.

Some suffering is avoidable and some is not. What is important is that we avoid fostering self-love in our sufferings by seeking abundant consolation, indulging in self-pity or by believing our sufferings make us worthy of special consideration. The best way to suffer is in silence and alone with God — Our Divine Physician. Suffering is a miraculous want which, by breaking the hardened and cold hearts, brings forth from it torrents of life and sanctity. It is suffering that makes us penetrate the profound secrets of the wisdom of God. **Suffering sums up all the blessings of earth.**

Prayer

Dear Father, through your Son Jesus, help me to be patient towards all, especially to you and myself. I truly want to learn to love sanctity and by that willingly carry my cross each day. I do not ask You to relieve me of my cross but to only give me the strength to bear it, silently and in patience. I wish to die to myself in all things that are not of You and from You. Amen

Resolution

I will offer all my suffering, whether spiritual, mental or physical, to your suffering on the Cross, dear Jesus, for souls, and to be used as you wish and for whom you wish. I willingly, with your help, will carry my crosses this day, knowing that I do not carry them alone, as you did, but that you are there to help me in every need. Help me to suffer all in joy, knowing that it will help in the salvation of my soul and the souls of others.

Meditations for March

A Cup of Blessing – Suffering and The Cross

"This treasure we possess in earthen vessels, to make it clear that Its surpassing power comes from God and not from us. We are afflicted in every way possible, but we are not crushed: full of doubts, we never despair. We are persecuted but never abandoned; we are struck down but never destroyed. Continually we carry about in our bodies the dying of Jesus, so that in our bodies the life of Jesus may also be revealed." (2 Corinthians 4:7-11)

March 1   Willingly Give of Self

(Jesus Speaks) Dear ones of My Sacred Heart, please continue to come daily and stay with Me, pray with Me, with Mary, with your Angels and Saints in front of My Blessed Sacrament. This is where graces flow for all the needs of today and the tomorrows to come. Learn how to imitate My ways, to willingly take up your crosses each day and to willingly give yourselves wholeheartedly to Me, to do with you as I will. Begin now to deny yourselves of little pleasures you have become accustomed to.

March 2   Follow the Savior

(Mary Speaks) My dearest children, stay always in the safe harbor of my heart. Keep focused on Jesus and on His

Cross at all times. Keep following only Jesus, My Son, through me and with me, through all the deception the world will afford. Dear ones, you are to follow only Him who is Savior and King, through Me, the Immaculate Virgin Mother. Follow Us through the giving of all you are and have, each day, to Us. This will mean you will travel up the Hill of Calvary, with me to My Son. In this walk you will travel with Me to Eternal Life.

March 3   (Feast – Blessed Katherine Drexel)
Worth of Sacrifice

(**Jesus Speaks**) My dear people, the Kingdom of Heaven is worth any sacrifice, any suffering in order to render one ready to approach the gate. I am the gate. I am the Narrow Path. I am your all, your only means to salvation, through the Heart of My Mother and the power of My Spirit. The power of grace to overcome temptation and struggle is victorious every time you ask for it. Remain in the shadow of My Cross, resting always in My Arms. Lean on My Mother. Cry out for Me to help you carry the crosses of self-denial and self-mortification that will over shadow self-centeredness.

March 4   (Feast – St. Casmir) Earthly Trials

(**Mary Speaks**) My loved ones, it is not easy to look beyond the feelings and attitudes of others. You must learn to do this and to practice unconditional love and gentleness. It is only love which can melt the hardness of Our children's hearts. Pray to your Angels to help and to remind you to offer each moment to Me, and I will purify each thought, act, and carry your pleas to My Son. **Each trial is a treasure being stored in Heaven for your return.**

March 5   Rejection and Focus

(**Jesus Speaks**) My little ones, you must not stand affronted when someone rejects or humbles you, for if you accept it as I would do and as I did, you will learn a great deal more on how self dies, much more than when someone flatters you. Focus yourself on Heaven through the Cross, on My Sacred and Merciful Heart, through Mary's Immaculate Heart and then **Be still and know that I am God...**

March 6   Strength to Carry Cross

(**St. Margaret Mary speaks**) Dear ones in His Sacred Heart, when you allow Jesus to venture into your heart from His Sacred Heart, and as you listen and begin to know in the silence of your heart, to recognize Him when He knocks, he will give you much strength to accept and to continue to carry the crosses He bestows on you. He gives you much enlightenment, help and courage. The heart then knows that He is there to help in the carrying of these crosses and that He would do anything to help you.

March 7   (Feast — Ss. Perpetua & Felicity)
Unconditional Yes

(**Mary Speaks**) My children, Jesus has shown through His Death, Resurrection and Ascension that He is the victor over death (sin) once and for all time. Jesus showed you that to die to sin is to say "yes" to Him, to the Father. When you give Him an unconditional yes, you have then said you would be willing to suffer as he suffered, to love as He loves, to take up your cross and follow Him on that rugged path leading to holiness, sanctity and His Divine Will. What joy awaits those souls who decide for this path of suffering, of letting God be God, to control them in all things.

March 8   (Feast — St. John of God) Defer to His Will

(**Mary Speaks**) My beloved children, no matter how you will ever have to suffer or are suffering, how or what you give up because of Him, deferring to His Will will bring much joy and peace. You will then know you are one with the Creator as was always planned. You will be able to look beyond the present circumstance and only see Paradise awaiting you. You will see Heaven with the eyes of the heart and the eyes of the soul. You will know that the reward awaiting far outweighs anything that can come or befall you in any way, while on this journey, to the Eternal Life of happiness.

March 9   (Feast — St. Frances of Rome)
        Carry Cross in Obedience

(**St. Francis of Assisi speaks**) Dear friends, there was much suffering in my life and there will be in yours, if you wish to truly follow Him. I carried my crosses in obedience, trust and love, in each direction He bade me go. All suffering and crosses are not of the physical kind. Those of the soul are sometimes more trying and painful. For whatever He wishes of you, pray for the grace to say "yes" to Him at every turn and to never look back. Never give in to the evil wiles of Lucifer and to the temptations he will throw in your path.

March 10   Becoming Human

(**Jesus Speaks**) Suffering, My children, is the vehicle by which My people become human. Their hard hearts are broken by certain events in their lives which cause great pain. This causes them to reflect in ways they never would otherwise. Pain breaks down defenses. Pain is felt in the deepest recesses of heart and soul. Nothing else will touch you at that depth. Joy is also felt deeply in your heart. This happens after the pain and suffering has broken open the ground of experience in order to receive the joy. Pain and grief drop seeds of joy, which bloom only after they are watered by the tears of remorse and repentance.

March 11   Unconditional Love

(**St. Francis of Assisi speaks**) My friends, even in the light of rejection, ridicule, pain and suffering, humiliation and many trials, you will learn unconditional love. Keep your eyes on His Cross, which is **THE CROSS**, as so much understanding will come to you when you open more to Him, giving all of you, your hearts, souls, wills. You will be following Him, living as He showed each of us by His own life while on earth.

March 12   Marks of Suffering

(**Jesus Speaks**) Dearest children, the more a soul resembles Me and contain the marks of My life, My suffering and death, the more like Me it will become in every way. Wounds and disease are caused by a split, a distance between the spiritual self and the worldly self. As long as this distance remains, wholeness and holiness cannot exist within that soul. The pride which exists in the hearts of mankind is the sign of Satan's continued presence. One is healed only by being patterned after My Life. This must happen for everyone before they can attain the salvation for which I died.

March 13   Contemplating the Cross

(**Jesus Speaks**) My beloved children, when you accept your own cross: your weakness, defects, ineptitude, incompleteness, pain and wounds, you can bring it to Me. I will press My Wounds against yours to heal them. You need do nothing but spend time with Me. Only in the silence of contemplating My Cross and your own crosses and offering them to Me in unity, will healing begin.

March 14   Love Sustains

(**Jesus Speaks**) Dear ones, My suffering and death were the result of My love for you. Your suffering and all the little deaths, (your crosses) are the result of My love for you, also. My love for you sustains you throughout your pain and suffering, just as My Father's love sustained Me. As you accept your life with its crosses, you will begin to discover the joy that can be yours in surrender.

March 15   Our Crosses

(**Jesus Speaks**) Dear ones of My Sacred Heart, carry your crosses always united with Mine. You will see how easy, though seemingly difficult, things will become. Know to offer all suffering in union with Mine, with My pain on the Cross and you will discover peace, joy and love. Follow My Cross, My Passion in your hearts often and you will know how to suffer as I did.

March 16   Hill to Calvary

(**Jesus Speaks**) My children, when you travel the hill to Calvary with Me, with My Mother, and stand beneath the Cross with her, immerse yourselves totally in Me, in My Passion and crucify yourselves with Me on that Cross. Die to yourselves that I may live totally in you and you may experience not only My Death and Passion, but also My Resurrection. Please come often to the Hill of Calvary with Mary.

March 17   (Feast — St. Patrick) Depth of Love

(**Jesus Speaks**) Beloved, many do not realize how great is the reward of the Cross. If you look up into My Heart, into My Eyes, you would see Heaven. You would see what Eternity would hold for those who willingly give all to Me. This is the choice each must make. No one, not even I, can make this choice for you.

March 18 (Feast — St. Cyril of Jerusalem)
Crossing the Threshold

(**Mary Speaks**) Children of My Immaculate Heart, always offer your crosses in union with Jesus' Cross. His Cross was and is the sign of love for all of us. Each of your crosses offered to Him and in union with Mine through Me, is your sign of love for Him. How this pleases Him. The path to Heaven, with Us in Eternity, is filled with suffering and sacrifices, but also filled with the joy of the crosses He allows each to carry. Crossing the threshold to the Kingdom can happen for you while still on earth.

March 19 (Feast — St. Joseph; Husband of Mary)
Great Graces at Foot of Cross

(**St. Joseph speaks**) My beloved children, I am honored today by all of you who celebrate this as a feast in my name. Thank you. I want to tell you of some things relating to Jesus' pain and suffering while on earth. His walk from the tiny crib in Bethlehem to the walk of Calvary He was to take some years later. This walk of His, of My Mary's, I watched even though I no longer was physically on earth with them. I prayed and cried silently because of Their pain. In all of this I gave thanks too, for our Father in Heaven, knowing if it had not been for Jesus, all of us would not have been able to enter into our eternal reward. Our salvation was won and the gates of Heaven were opened to us. It was bought by His Most Precious Blood.

Whenever pain or suffering comes into your life, do not be despondent or angry or questioning, no, always give praise and thanksgiving to Him Who knew pain and suffering as no one has ever known before, or will again. Unite all with Him for the salvation of souls. Be a co-redeemer with Him, with all of us who are unceasingly praying for souls. This is a great grace and privilege that the Father allows when one suffers for souls, in communion with the pain of His Son and His Death on the Cross of Calvary. Pray always to be given the grace to be able to stand at the foot of His Cross with Mary and pledge your undying love for Him, doing as He wills in you, at all times. Being united fully with Jesus and Mary is a gift of great value. Use it wisely and always return love for love.

March 20   Suffering of Others

(**Jesus Speaks**) Beloved children, when you focus on Me, on My Mother and on all the horrible sufferings of Our dear ones throughout the world, you will notice the difference between your life and theirs. Allow their pain and suffering to be the impetus for your industry on their behalf. Pray and lament for them, my children, as no prayer or effort is too small on behalf of My loved ones, who will remain feeling so devastated and alone.

March 21   Joy in Suffering

(**Jesus Speaks**) Beloved ones, think of nothing else save being with Me, walking in My love and sharing My thoughts and feelings. When a soul is in love, nothing is too good for or too great a task to perform for its beloved. Any suffering or hardship is considered no trial at all when it is performed at the request of the One Who is loved. The time spent serving the Beloved is a mere second on the clock of Eternal Love.

March 22   Look Straight Ahead

(**Mary Speaks**) Dearest children, do not ever change your focus. Keep looking straight ahead to the Cross and why Jesus did what He did for each of you; why the Father asked His only Son to do what was done for you. Do not lose sight of this now or ever. The path to Heaven with Us in Eternity is rough and narrow, filled with suffering and sacrifices. It is also filled with hope and joy over the crosses He allows each of you to carry. You will be filled with praise and thanksgiving in this joy of your crosses. Empty yourselves completely so He can fill you with Himself and with the graces necessary to arrive at the next crossroads, which is upon you.

March 23   Stop and Listen

(**Jesus Speaks**) My children, prepare yourselves for anything the Father has planned for you. Stop and listen to your hearts always. You must learn to live My mercy and be in My Will, forsaking all for Me, letting go of self, taking up your cross every day and carrying it with Me, to a complete spiritual union between My Heart and yours. If what you are doing is not leading to the salvation of your soul and the souls of others, beware.

March 24   To Gain Salvation

(**Mary Speaks**) Dear ones, when you accept being consecrated to Jesus through My Immaculate Heart, you are then called to live a holy life through this consecration. This is teaching you to keep focused on The Cross at all times. This is perhaps the easiest and surest way of gaining the salvation for your soul. The hard part is giving up what the world has to offer. It is a total giving, a total commitment, and a total dying to self. Die to self you must, so you can die with Him. Take up your crosses and follow Him.

March 25   (Feast of Annunciation of the Lord) The Way

(**Mary Speaks**) Dear children, allow me to bring you to the foot of the Cross, as once I brought you to Bethlehem at the birth of our Savior, My Son, Jesus. This was all in keeping with the plan of the Father from the Annunciation. Allow me now to show you the depths of my love, as I followed my Jesus from a distance, through the street lined with shouting, jeering people whose only thoughts were to kill my Jesus. Allow the feelings to penetrate your heart, as you hear these sounds and terrible words. See what they are doing to Him Whom I love. See how they push and taunt Him. I long to run to Him and shield His bruised Body with my own. But I must stay away and allow all of Scripture to be fulfilled. All of Heaven contemplates the beginning of My Son's Passion. You will be more surely united with me if you walk this **WAY** in my company. **Join me now children, as we walk the streets behind Him and watch Him suffer and die.**

March 26   Mother's Support

(**Jesus Speaks**) My people, do you ever wonder what it was like for Me in the days before going up to Jerusalem to begin My Passion and ultimate death? I had no true support other than My Mother, who understood completely what must occur. It was her love and encouragement that allowed Me to wait, to continue one day, one step at a time the Path to Calvary. Being human, I was assailed by temptations to flee, to escape, to impatience, to despair. Flee to My Mother, dear ones. Escape into her Immaculate Heart. Bring all to her. I tell you this gave Me much strength and courage to be able to follow that Path, but more importantly, to wait for the actual day decreed by My Father, for it to begin.

March 27   Hill of Shame

(**Jesus Speaks**) Walk with Me, dearest children, carry My Cross with Me. Fall with Me and rise again to continue to the **Hill of Shame**. It is only a matter of moments now before My Passion begins. Won't you join Me every step of the way and find out how much I love you now and how much I loved you then? If you look at Me on that Cross, you will be able to see My undying love for each of you. Keep your focus on Me and a good balance between heaven and earth. I leave you My peace, love, and mercy in all hearts that have opened to Me, to My Words, to My Church and to all My children. I love and **am Love. Please love Love in return.**

March 28   The Lamb

(**Mary Speaks**) Dearest ones of My Sorrowful Heart: My Son, the Lamb, must be slain for the very people who are screaming for His death. He must be slain for you too, my beloved children. They are intent on destroying the One Who has loved and served them, taught and healed them and Who only wished to bring them knowledge of the Father and His great love for them. Can you bear to watch this scene, children of mine? Can you bear to see His Sacred Blood poured out on the filthy street to mingle with the dust and the dirt?

March 29   To the Foot of the Cross

(**Jesus Speaks**) Loved ones, when My children bring souls you pray for and give them to My Mother who stands beneath the Cross, she will enclose these souls in Her Immaculate Heart and offer them to Me. You then have taken the first step for those you pray for. It is then up to them to take the next and final steps to come to Me here, beneath the Cross and express their love, their repentance for all their sins. Pray children, that they will embrace My Cross, as they willingly give themselves to Me through Mary, the Immaculate One, here at the **Foot of the Cross.**

March 30   Time to Come

(**Jesus Speaks**) My dear children, there will come a time when all of you, in some way or another, will suffer. Some will suffer more than others for the salvation of souls. Some will see the Father's plan unfold in their hearts: this will happen in hearts that will be open to Him. This can only be done in close union with Me and with Mary, your Mother. Follow My Cross, My Passion in your hearts often and you will then know how to suffer as I did.

March 31   My Passion and Yours

(Jesus Speaks) My beloved ones, it is now moments away from My Crucifixion. Become acutely aware of all I endured for you. Become one with Me for this brief period of time so that I can show you all the things you wish to know, so that I can give you a drink from My Cup, so that I can sign you with the sign of My suffering. Come now and be lifted up with Me. Hang on My Cross and die with Me, in perfect union with My Will for you. You will be Mine forever, as We become more completely united. It is this I have created you for. It is now all according to the Father's Will.

APRIL

Eucharist/Mercy and Love

"God is love, and he who abides in love abides in God and God in him. Our love is brought to perfection in this, that we should have confidence on the Day of Judgment; for our relation to this world is just like His. Love has no room for fear; rather, perfect love casts out all fear. And since fear has to do with punishment, love is not yet perfect in one who is afraid." (1 John 4:16-19)

Mercy: Mercy is the greatest attribute of God. The essence of mercy is trust. God's mercy is unconditional love and forgiveness, but after our first encounter, it is conditional. We receive mercy and then, as we hear in the Lord's prayer, we must have mercy on others in order to receive it. Our Holy Father, Pope John Paul, wrote an encyclical, "Rich in Mercy" wherein he states, **"the concept of mercy is almost absent from the heart of the 'world' which has become master of**

the earth, subduing and dominating it. It is important to find the God of mercy as presented in the Old Testaments and in the New; to have recourse to that mercy and to reflect on it..."

Pope John Paul goes on to say: "Through the parable of the Prodigal Son, we see a son, who rebelled and sinned against the father, is still a son! We are all invited to this. Conversion is the most concrete expression of the working of love and the presence of mercy in the human world. Mercy is the mission of the Church. She must bear witness to the mercy of God, revealed in Christ: to introduce it and make it incarnate in the lives of both her faithful and as far as possible, in people of good will..."

Reflection for the Month

Adoration/Eucharist: When you are in adoration, you are uniting yourself with Jesus and Mary on Calvary, then all the Father can say is YES to what is asked of Him in His Son's Name and in His Will and in His Precious Blood. What a treasure you then have for souls, as everything is brought before the throne of the Most High. If you could but know how love and mercy flow out to souls, as grace, as merits, as a crown, to souls, you would come often to Him, praising Him, giving all to Him, especially your wills. This is the greatest gift you can give back to Him, as then love becomes complete. He can, as you can, truly say your hearts are one.

Remember when we receive the Sacred Host, Christ is Alive. Christ is not alone. The Trinity is present there united with Him. Christ is **totally present in the Eucharist with-**

out ever leaving Heaven. We know this because He told us that He and the Father are one. There is only ONE MASS, and Christ is celebrating IT and IT is going on all the time in the Eternal NOW!

Divine Mercy: Jesus has said, *"through My Crucifixion and Death and then My Resurrection; all this becomes the walk of My Divine Mercy and leads you to the great feast of My Divine Mercy. If you were to learn anything from this regarding your reflection on this, you need to walk in My footsteps to Calvary. You need to say as I did, 'Father forgive them for they know not what they do…' You need to love each other as I love you. Without this, you cannot possibly love Me or love the Father and Creator of all. It starts with being able to forgive, to accept forgiveness, to forget once you have forgiven and have been forgiven. Then look at each other with the eyes of love, with My Eyes and Heart and you will see My reflection in all you meet, in all you do. You will be walking in My walk, the walk of forgiveness, to love and mercy."*

Prayer

Dear Heart of My Merciful Lord and Savior, help me, through your love and mercy, to have Love conquer me completely, and have It possess my heart always. I know that you have shown me how to conform my life to Yours, and that love means suffering in union with your suffering, please give me the grace to realize this fully in my life, that I may truly do everything through love and for love, making good use of the present moment and not to be anxious about the future. Amen

Resolution

This month I will make it a point to go regularly to the Holy Sacrifice of the Mass, as often as every day, my daily duty permitting. I will give to the Lord the first fruits of my day, by spending an hour with Him, before Him, in adoration, in front of the Blessed Sacrament. I will be mercy as He is mercy to my brothers and sisters, to myself and to Him, my God. I will unite myself in all that I think, say and do with Jesus for the honor and glory of the Father.

Note: Recommend reading and contemplating Pope John Paul II's encyclical letter, "The Mercy of God" (*Dires in Misericordia*) as well as *The Return of the Prodigal Son* by Fr. Henri J.M. Nouwen.

Meditations for April

Eucharist / Mercy and Love

"How lovely is Your dwelling place, O Lord of hosts! My soul yearns and pines for the courts of the Lord. My heart and my flesh cry out for the living God." (Psalm 84:2-4)

April 1   Heart to Heart

(Jesus speaks) My beloved children, please bring all to Me, always, in front of the Blessed Sacrament. It is there you will find peace and quiet, in the solitude of Our Hearts; Our Hearts to your hearts and your hearts to Our Hearts. Answers will be forthcoming then. You will know by the grace given what is from Us, what is Our Wish and Will in all you do, when you do this. Do all in the State of Grace at all times.

April 2   (Feast — St. Francis of Paola) I am Here

(Jesus speaks) Children of My Heart, it saddens My Heart to know of the many who do not believe (of the believers) in My Real Presence there on your altars and in your Tabernacles. Believe in faith that when you receive Me in Communion you are receiving My Body, Blood, Soul and Divinity. This is TRUTH for **I am!** Come often to My Cross, to My Altar of Sacrifice, to the Eucharist. Come as often as your daily duty will permit. Come to be with me and visit with Me, in My Blessed Sacrament. Do not put any unnecessary strain on your families, as there will open up opportunities of grace for you to be able to come to Me.

April 3   Prepare to Meet Him

(**Mary speaks**) My dearest children, before the Mass, please be in prayer recollection before you receive the King of Kings into your hearts and souls. It is so pleasing to Him when you come a little early to prepare your whole self before Him in adoration, in repentance of any offenses, asking His forgiveness and asking the Holy Spirit to prepare your soul for this most important encounter of your life. Those who do not prepare miss so much. Do not ignore the fact that a most wonderful encounter is about to take place, between man and God on that Altar, during the Consecration, when He allows Himself to humbly come to you, under the species of bread and wine. Then it is no longer a species but truly your Jesus, complete in His Body, Blood, Soul and Divinity.

April 4   (Feast – St. Isidore of Seville, Bishop/Doctor) Reverence

(**Mary speaks**) My loved ones, so many are no longer reverent when they come to visit with Him (Jesus), when they are about to receive His Word and His Precious Body and Blood. How can one prepare properly for this Precious Treasure when there is constant talking and chatter before the Mass? How can you contemplate Who it is you have come to see and visit when you are thinking of so many other things. How can anything be more important than preparing for the visitor of a lifetime? Please save the chatter for afterwards, outside. Our God is a selfish God. He wants you for Himself, especially at that very special time. And, He wants you to want Him in the same manner.

April 5   (Feast — St. Vincent Ferrer)
Brilliance of His Being

(**Jesus speaks**) Dearest ones of My Sacred Heart, when you look at Me in the Tabernacle and realize that My Real Presence is before you, that I am here, this is as much as most human beings can afford. As you look at Me, I look at you with much love. If I were to reveal My Presence to you, more so, My Light would more than make you immobile. You would not be able to see for the brilliance of My Being, and would be blinded at such intense light and beauty. **My Presence is Real in The Tabernacle!**

April 6   Praise and Thanksgiving

(**Mary speaks**) Beloved children, before and after the Mass I would suggest you take time first to visit with Jesus, to prepare before and then to praise and thank Him after the Mass, before you do anything else. This is a special time between your soul and your Creator, your Jesus. You need that time alone with Him, just to be in silent adoration of Him, your Heavenly Guest, whom you now have captive. He has come to visit you and you alone. Treat Him as you would a king, for loved ones, that is exactly what He is. He is your King, your Beloved, Who loves you so completely as to retreat into your house (heart/soul), to love you, to heal you, to hold you, to bring you a peace you can find nowhere else.

April 7   (Feast — St. John Baptist De La Salle)
              One Hour a Day

(**Mary speaks**) Children of My Immaculate Heart, if you cannot come to Eucharistic Adoration of My Son, then come at least one hour a day before Him in the Blessed Sacrament in the Tabernacle. Sit in silence in His Presence. When you come to see Him, I am also always there, at His side, by His Tabernacle. You will then see wonders happen and healing will come. He wants to strengthen you through this gift of Himself, so your hearts, souls and bodies will be filled with grace to always be ready for whatever the Father has planned for you.

April 8   Purity of Heart

(**Mary speaks**) My loved little ones, always have purity of heart so you will be able to see God in all you do and in all you meet. There must be love, my children. Without love there will never be unity and without unity you do not have God. The lesson is so simple: faith, trust, love, conversion, all through prayer, prayer that will bring peace and purity of heart, mind and soul.

April 9   Come to Mercy and Love

(**Jesus speaks**) Dear ones, I will remember My Holy Covenant that I make with you, to save this errant people of the world, if they but listen to My pleas and come to My Mercy and Love. Serve Me all the days of your lives and be holy in My Sight. I am the Day Spring and My mercy is visiting My people to let them know of My love. I plead with you to continue spreading My mercy, My Father's mercy and to live mercy in your lives every day. My children, please remember My mercy is love. When you trust and completely submit everything to Me, turning your entire lives and beings over to Me, you begin to live in My Mercy and My Will. As you will, your will, to be Mine completely, you please Me because of your undaunted love and mercy shown Me in return. To become perfect as I am perfect, as Our Heavenly Father is perfect, should always be something to strive for in your lives. Understand My Mercy, My love and then live this in your every day lives. **Your very lives depend on this.** It depends on a faith so unshakable, so powerful, that the strongest hurricane could not move you.

April 10   Silence

(**Jesus speaks**) My dear ones, you must spend more time in silence before Me and allow Me to heal you. **Avoid all that would disturb your spirit for your own sake.** Dwell in Me, in My Sacred Heart. You are safe in the silence of My Presence. Have no fear in My Presence. Do you not know that what the world has to offer is but illusion and is passing away? Why do you continue to look in the wrong places and in the wrong direction? **I am here, in your Tabernacles and in the Communion you receive.** Please do not refuse Me entrance into your lives.

April 11   (Feast — St. Stanislaus of Cracow)
Living Examples

(**Jesus speaks**) My beloved children, please pray with Me for My children who have strayed from My Sheepfold. Offer them insights into My love and mercy. Be My Light as you shine, showing them Me, by your living examples of trust, love and mercy. We are inviting all of you to be Our prophets, Our disciples of mercy and love. All of you have been given many gifts and graces. Please use them to proclaim My mercy.

April 12   No Boundaries

(**Jesus speaks**) Beloved ones, if you believe in My mercy, it will be freely given to you and to all for whom you ask it. My mercy knows no boundaries. The times in which you live and the influence of the evil one can only be countered by My grace and mercy. Pray that you and those you pray for will accept the graces and mercy being offered to you. Remember, My children, **I am Love, Mercy, Compassion and Gentleness.** I am all a soul needs. Use Me as I want to give and give and give some more.

April 13   (Feast — St. Martin I, Pope)
Father's Love and Mercy

(**Jesus speaks**) My children, the cup of My mercy, My love, My Heart never runs dry. Drink from this Cup. This is where your thirst and hunger will be satisfied. This is where you will find peace. Please, dear ones, ponder the greatness of My Father's love and the gifts and mercy He has for you. It is the way to holiness. It is the means to the perseverance you desire. The ability to serve faithfully does not happen, is not given all at once: It is built and it develops day by day.

April 14   Happy the Heart

(St. Margaret Mary speaks) My dear brothers and sisters in His Sacred and Merciful Heart, the more times you come to adore Him in His Sacred Presence, whether in front of Him in the Blessed Sacrament or through Perpetual Eucharistic Adoration, or receiving Him in Holy Communion, you will begin to realize the gift He has given to all of mankind; the precious gift of His Real Presence among men. How happy the heart, the soul is, who believes in His Real Presence in the Eucharist.

It gives all of Heaven a delight beyond words to see you come to Him, in your nothingness and in humility, trusting that He is indeed with you and among you and will be until the end of time. To love as He loves is what all souls, all hearts should desire and strive for. He has taken on a smallness in His humility to be hidden there in the Blessed Sacrament, in that little Host you receive in Communion and in the Host you see in the Monstrance. He does this because of His undying love for you, His beloved children.

April 15   Divine Presence

(Mary speaks) My little children, bring more people to the knowledge of My Son through the Sacrament of His Divine Presence on the Altar at the Consecration when He transforms the host and the wine into His Precious Body and Blood, His Real Presence with you. Jesus needs your prayers and your adoration. He especially needs that time alone with you when you visit Him in the Blessed Sacrament. When you open your hearts to Him, He can do much for you. Children, you are a Eucharistic people. Do not forget this. Being in His Eucharistic Presence, adoring and praising Him is very important to your spiritual growth. This is where you are nourished, where you are fed the bread of life, by Jesus, your God, by His love and His mercy. Do you really believe in His Real Presence? Do you know the treasure of what you have before you? Please come to Us, in front of the Blessed Sacrament, where answers are given through inspirations from Our Hearts to your hearts. Miracles then happen.

April 16   Apostles of Mercy

(**Mary speaks**) My beloved children, pray many prayers to the Holy Spirit. Invoke His grace, His gifts on you. In this way you will feel the urgency to become an Apostle of Mercy, an Apostle of Prayer and Apostles of the Most Holy Eucharist. You then will be filled with the desire to spend more time with Us in adoration. The Holy Spirit then can feed you, give you the grace needed to go out as His Apostles to tell of the immediate need for all to come to Him in this Blessed Sacrament, where He waits for each with a hunger and love that surpasses anything you can imagine.

April 17   Miracles

(**Mary speaks**) Children of My Immaculate Heart, through Jesus' Precious Blood and through Perpetual Adoration, many miracles happen and will continue to happen. Adoration of Him and believing in His Real Presence is what will bring my children, His children, back to Him and to His Church. Many conversions will then be seen. Your Churches will overflow. If only you would come and acknowledge Him as King of Kings Lord of Lords, your God and Savior, Who is the only means of salvation. I am the Mother of The Eucharist. I am His Holy Mother. I am always at His side next to each Tabernacle, each Monstrance, adoring and pleading for my children.

April 18   Be Refreshed

(**Jesus speaks**) My loved children, come to Me in the Blessed Sacrament to be refreshed, to seek shelter, to know how to find love and then give it to others. This pleases Me. Come to Me in the Eucharist, as I cannot dwell any closer than when I am with you, through your receiving My Body and Blood in Communion. You are then filled by the **Spring of Life** and have that **Blessed Manna** that only I can give to nourish the soul and the body.

April 19   Grace Through Faith

(**Jesus speaks**) Dear children of My Eucharistic Heart, did you know angels surround the Tabernacle in your churches? They surround the Monstrance of Exposition and sing out their alleluias in praise and thanksgiving for this union of hearts, man's heart to God's Heart. Graces come doubly to a soul who believes I am present even though not seen. You then see Me with your heart. What Joy!!

April 20   Peace

(**Jesus speaks**) Dear ones, My Presence in the Host is Real. My Presence is Divine, is Human, for **I AM! I AM** and always will be here for you who come to be refreshed. This is My gift of love to you. Your peace, joy and love come from being in My Presence. I take all who come to adore and love Me into the deepest recesses of My Heart. Listen for My beckoning in the silence of that place that is Mine in your heart, where My Mother and I take comfort. Remain in stillness and in peace, so you will never miss an opportunity of Our being with you and conversing with you.

April 21 (Feast — St. Anselm, Bishop/Doctor)
Hunger for God

(**Jesus speaks**) My dearest ones, when you feel the hunger to come to Me, to see Me, to be with Me, to adore and love Me, in the Blessed Sacrament, you then begin to understand how much I have to give, how far reaching My love, My mercy is and always has been and always will be. When you look at Me and I at you, the energy, the fire that consumes your soul is complete. Then, as you allow Me to completely wrap Myself in you, in your heart, I unite your heart with Mine. This then is a complete trust on the part of man for their God, through Me in this Blessed Sacrament.

April 22 Love Me Always

(**Jesus speaks**) My dearest children, love Me always and in all ways, not only when you need something. I know your hearts. I know your needs. I answer your heart prayers, for you are Mine. All are Mine who are consecrated to Me through My Mother's Immaculate Heart. I, your Lord, wait for you always to come. Do not ever feel lonely or alone; run to Me

Who awaits your company and your love, with love. I am always with you. You have only to pause to notice My Presence. If you are constantly living in My Presence, you cannot feel lonely or unloved.

April 23   (Feast — Ss. George & Adalbert) Greatest Gift

(**Jesus speaks**) Precious children of My Sacred Heart; To sit in My Presence is your greatest gift as a member of My Body! It is the Will of My Father that all His creatures adore Me and love Me by sharing these silent hours with Me. I am indeed a prisoner for love of My children. If you would only realize that this is not a chore, but a blessing, a time for healing and strengthening. There will never be anything you can do which would help to heal, to strengthen you, like the power of just being with Me and visiting with Me in front of My Blessed Sacrament. Please continue to come to Me and make My Presence your home.

April 24   (Feast — St. Fidelis of Sigmaringen)
Breathe in Grace

(**Jesus speaks**) My dearest ones, when you come to adore Me, breathe deeply of the sanctity here before you in My Sacred Eucharist, this holy Sacrament of My Presence, this beloved gift of My Father, to all of you. Soak up, bathe in the Sacrament of My Love for you. See the longing in My Eyes and feel the tenderness of My Heart. Nowhere else is this available to My people who wish to be close to Me, in the oneness of My Blessed Trinity. Please give proper thanks and praise to Him Who loves and blesses you to this degree.

April 25 (Feast — St. Mark, Evangelist) Present Moment

(**Jesus speaks**) My beloved, please stay in the present moment in a deeper awareness of My Presence and be comforted by a knowledge of My Love. The heart grows impatient when it is not at rest. The Heart cannot be at rest when it is consumed with questioning and requests. Be content with what is and know that this contentment is the only way you can be aware of My Presence and love for you. Seek Me in peace and docility. Be content with My desires for your future and what this will mean for you. You have the opportunity of being renewed by My Hand, if only you will ask for My forgiveness and pledge to Me your sorrow and eagerness to repent.

April 26 (Feast — Our Lady of Good Counsel) Living Mercy

(**Jesus speaks**) Dear children of My Heart, many need to see how mercy can work in their lives. Mercy needs to be lived and should be practiced in your lives by forgiveness. All of you need My healing touch which is My mercy and love. This I give most effectively through My Sacraments of Reconciliation and Eucharist. You must forgive. That is mercy and love. That is living mercy. Go back to the table of the Lord, work together for the good of all and not just the few.

April 27 Much to be Gained

(**Mary speaks**) My precious children, much can be gained by coming every day in front of Him in the Blessed Sacrament or in Eucharistic Adoration and receiving Him in the Sacraments of the Euchrist and of Reconciliation. Then all guile, all pride, all anger, all ego, all self would be lost and only He would remain, would exist in each soul. It is then peace would reign in hearts, in families, in nations, in countries and in the world. Through prayer, all will realize again **His Real Presence** among you. You will realize love and mercy and how it is to be shared.

April 28 (Feast — Ss. Louis de Monfort & Peter Chanel) Oneness with God

(Jesus speaks) Listen and respond, My dear ones, with all your hearts. Come away with Me at every opportunity for prayer and quiet. Learn more about My love by absorbing it in the silence. Sit before Me and gaze at My loving Heart. Adore Me in the hidden-ness of My Sacrament before you on the Altar. Become one with Me. This is accomplished by the two of us being alone so we can absorb each other's being, presence, essence: The true knowledge of My Selfhood is perceived by gazing, listening, contemplating and reflecting. The mystery of our oneness can only be explained once it is experienced and then, it is a matter of degrees and increases. It is My greatest desire to be more intimately united to you, to have you melt into Me.

April 29 (Feast — St. Catherine of Siena) Banquet in The Kingdom

(Mary speaks) My beloved children, the Eucharist should be the center of your lives. Here is Jesus: He is alive and present to you, there in the Blessed Sacrament. The Tabernacle holds His Precious Body, Blood, Soul and Divinity. He is truly present, as I am present with you. Where He is in all the Tabernacles of the world, there I am as well. You will find hundreds of Angels in constant and continuous adoration before Him in that Tabernacle. My children, you must be centered on Him in the Eucharist. Come and feast on goodness and mercy at the banquet of His Kingdom. All are invited, but so few come. Continue on the road that leads to Our Hearts and to doing His Will through me, His Mother. Come to the front where you will see the glorious Reign of your King. Always praise and thank the Triune God for everything.

April 30   (Feast — Our Lady of Consolation & St. Pius V, Pope) Unfathomable Love

(**Jesus speaks**) Children of My Sacred and Merciful Heart, I love each of you so very much and would certainly die again, a death even a thousand times more insidious, if it were possible for just one soul to be saved. This is how much I love. My Love is unfathomable and cannot be understood by the human mind and heart. One must just accept in faith and trust that this love, this mercy, will never change. Love is a gift of God, dear ones. If you had not received this from him when you became His child, you would be walking and stumbling around in complete darkness. Trust in your Jesus and in His Divine Mercy. I am Jesus Who is Love and Power that created the universe and everyone in it. I am the One Who has promised to save you. Be no longer afraid. I am unchangeable because **I AM,** and always will be. **God is Love. I AM LOVE, FOR I AM GOD!**

MAY

Mother of God and Our Mother – Total Consecration

"Seeing His Mother there with the disciple whom He loved, Jesus said to His Mother, 'Woman, there is your son.' In turn, he said to the disciple, 'There is your mother.' From that hour onward, the disciple took her into his care." (John 19:26-27)

The most holy Virgin, Holy Mary, is given to us as the Masterpiece of the Father's mercy. For God's love to be communicated to us, there must be a bridge and that bridge is Mary. We know that a gift is always meant to be shared with others. It is for others, not to be kept for ourselves. Are you sharing Mary? Try to realize that in Mary there is a magnificent palace built of gold and precious stones, worthy of the great King Who dwells there and then try to realize what is true: that you are contributing toward His splendor and glory by honoring His permanent dwelling place, which is the Immaculate Heart of Mary. Through Mary's obedience was decided the work of Redemption and was espoused by the Holy Spirit. Mary is the Immaculate, the direct way to Christ, the weapon of conquest with which to establish the reign of Jesus Christ from one end of the earth to the other.

Mary is the purity of the Father's mercy; there is no mercy more absolute nor complete in a human creature. Mary is the one who received mercy in a particular, personal, exceptional and unique way, as no other person ever has. When we consecrate in this act of submission to Jesus through Mary, it allows us to draw nearer to the fountain of mercy that Mary is. She, like her Son, is all merciful.

Reflection for the Month

The Blessed Mother has said, "The door that opens directly to Jesus' Sacred Heart, to His mercy, love and grace, is My Immaculate Heart. It has always been that way and shall continue to be. That is why it is so necessary, so very important that more know of consecrating their lives to Him, through me. This is no longer an option. It is now a necessity! Dear ones, I am the Mediatrix of all grace, so I know how to take a soul and show it how to please Our God by giving it to His Son, to My Son, Jesus, in complete surrender and consecration to His Mercy and to His Sacred Heart. Once united to Jesus through me, the path is cleared of any and all obstacles to reach the Throne of the Most High God, the Father, Who loves with incomprehensible tenderness all His creatures, you His children."

The greatest truth about Mary is that she is the Mother of God, "*Theotokos*," the God bearer. All her graces and privileges are for, or are, from her Motherhood. Pope John Paul's

"Mother of the Redeemer" was written to prepare for the New Advent of 2000. He shows that Mary's characteristics are to be those of the Church: Faith, Grace, Pilgrimage, Union with God, Mediation, Unity and Eucharist.

Entrustment to Mary is then the fulfillment of the command of Jesus: "Behold your Mother." When you have consecrated you hearts to Jesus through Mary's Immaculate Heart, your responsibility to Them begins and increases because you are then totally Mary's, under the protection of her mantle. The door that opens directly to Jesus' Heart, to His mercy and grace, is and always will be, through the Immaculate Heart of Mary. As you consecrate daily your entire selves, you will receive graces and blessings, to be able to do, in wisdom and courage, what needs to be done each day for Them.

Prayer

Dearest Mother, take me directly to your Son, Jesus, through your Immaculate Heart, where I find in your heart, the refuge, the courage, the strength, the humility and obedience to always do His Will in all, through you.

Resolution

I want to know the Most Holy Trinity more intimately, which I will do by consecrating myself to you, dearest Mother Mary. Through your Immaculate Heart I will find the love and refuge, the safe harbor, that only can be found in the Hearts of God the Father, God the Son and God the Holy Spirit.

Meditations for May

Mother of God and Our Mother – Total Consecration

> "The angel went on to say to her: 'Do not fear, Mary, You have found favor with God. You shall conceive and bear a son and give him the name, Jesus…' Mary treasured all these things and reflected on them in her heart." (Luke 1:30-31 and Luke 2:19)

May 1   (Feast – St. Joseph the Worker)
       Run to My Arms

(**Mary speaks**) Loved ones of My Immaculate Heart, am I not your mother? Am I not here for you who call on me? My wish is that more would run to my arms, to my heart, as this is where you find shelter, peace, love and mercy. I want to love all my children back to health (spiritual health). Come, for I am always here. I want to mother all of you back to Him, the most loving of Fathers, Who waits for your return. Pray for continued grace in perseverance and trust and an unshakable faith. Keep a tight hold of my hand and stay under the protection of my mantle and within the refuge of My Immaculate Heart.

May 2   (Feast – St. Athanasius, Bishop/Doctor)
       Mirror Image

(**Jesus speaks**) Beloved children, your hearts are to be a complete mirror image of My Heart through My Mother's

Immaculate Heart. Give all to her always, for she knows what and how to care for your hearts and souls. From her heart all roads lead to Mine and when you are in her heart, you are in Mine. Come always to Me, to the Holy Spirit through Mary's Immaculate Heart. She is Our Love. The Father chose her from the beginning of time to be My Mother, to be your Mother and to be the Blessed Spouse of Our Holy Spirit.

May 3 (Feast — Ss. Philip and James, Apostles) Ask for Mary's Spirit

(Mary speaks) My dearest children, you are wise and prudent to continue to ask me to pray with you and for you, giving all to My Immaculate Heart. All that comes to My Heart goes to His Divine and Merciful and Sacred Heart. Continue to ask me for my spirit while you reject your spirit (the spirit of the world). When you ask for my spirit, your whole being is being saturated with me and the grace I have been given to give you, His children, you who ask for it. When you have my spirit, you have the Spirit of the Triune Godhead. When you have me entirely within you, you have asked to have the complete indwelling of the Most Holy Trinity. What more could you ever need?

May 4 Vessels of your Souls

(Mary speaks) Beloved ones, you who consecrate your-selves to me, to My Immaculate Heart, are automatically given to My Jesus, for His tender love and mercy, all for the well-being of your hearts, souls and bodies. You are then "wholly and completely" one with Us, with Our Sacred Hearts. My love is constantly being poured into the vessels of your souls, with the grace that is much needed now and in the days that lie ahead. Pray to the Holy Spirit always, for all the gifts and graces They have planned for you. My children, all of you have a great need for these graces and gifts.

May 5   Your "Yes"

(**Mary speaks**) My littlest ones, **I am your mother** and I will take care of all who are mine, who are consecrated to me, to Jesus. through me. Your fiats, saying yes, are important to be joined with mine, so I can place them all in My Immaculate Heart and give them to His Sacred Heart as testimony that you now belong to Him through me. Through my heart many doors open in the Kingdom. So come, come and partake of all the gifts that await each of you.

May 6   The Plan

(**Jesus speaks**) Dear ones of My Sacred Heart, it is well you ask My Mother to always give you her spirit to live and breathe in you. You will need her courage, her gentleness, her attitude of peace and love, so she can work My Plan in your lives, for the salvation of your soul and all souls. As you consecrate your beings to Me through My Immaculate Mother, each day, your entire selves, you will receive graces and blessings to be able to do in wisdom and courage what needs doing each day for Us. You can go out fearlessly doing the work which will be expected of you. You will never be alone.

May 7   Our Lady of Good Counsel

(**Mary speaks**) My sweet ones, when you have decided to give me your spirits by rejection of your spirits, asking for my spirit, I would also invite you to ask for my dispositions. Ask for my thoughts, my desires, my feelings. Say often the prayer to **"Our Lady of Good Counsel."** I will guide and direct each of you through this prayer as I counsel you.

> Prayer: **"Mary, I renounce my spirit and I ask for your spirit. Mary take away My thoughts and give me your thoughts. Mary, take away my desires and give me Your desires. Mary take away my feelings, and give me your feelings. I am totally Yours and everything I have I offer you, O my beloved Jesus, through Mary Your Most Holy Mother. Come Holy Spirit, come by means of the powerful intercession Of the Immaculate Heart of Mary, Your well beloved Spouse. (Then say three Hail Mary's Repeating after each, 'Mother of Good Counsel give us good counsel.') Amen"**

May 8   Mary's Presence With Us

(**Mary speaks**) Dear children of Mine, I would wish for you to practice praying with me and to me and thinking of me at every moment. You will be calmed and quieted in this way, my children. You will be molded and formed in my image very quickly, if you allow me to be present to you at all times. My presence will change you; it will strengthen you and will keep you close to me and to My Son. Please try again and again to do this, as it will be very difficult to accomplish. With practice and the help of my Spouse, the Holy Spirit, you will make great progress. Invite me to be with you and pray with you at each moment of your day.

May 9   Teacher and Guide

(**Jesus speaks**) My beloved children, follow My Mother. Listen closely to her, for she will bring you to My Sacred Heart each moment of the day. Be united with her in prayer and love. Allow her to be your teacher and guide. Stand by her in the dark days that will come into your lives at times. Be a beacon of truth for all who will seek Me. Bring Our lost little ones to her, your Mother, and then together, bring them to Me. I await you in My Blessed Sacrament. I long for My children to return to Me.

May10   My Mother

(**Jesus speaks**) Dearly loved ones, My Mother is very special! Follow her manner. Learn her gentleness. Be aware of the gentleness with which she accepts all who come to her, how she calms fears and tenderly wipes away tears. Be still and listen to the soothing tones of her voice, the melody of love which sings from her heart. In the warmth of the smile of My Mother, all is well. In the Shadow of her Mantle, we are favored. The love of My Mother will bring mankind to their knees to honor and adore the One, True, Living God. It is My Mother who will bring the lost sheep back to the fold.

It is she who loves Me so much and soothes the grief I feel for My lost ones who reject Me.

May 11   Acknowledge the Mother

(**Mary speaks**) Beloved children, My triumph is here and is continuing in the hearts and souls of those who acknowledge me and this triumph will be completed when your soul realizes who you are and what you owe your Creator. In the fullness of time, in the new era, His Reign will come with my triumph and His glorious Second Coming will be felt and seen by all. His Second Coming will be triumphant and glorious. Praise and thank Him for everything, for soon His glory will be known to all.

May 12   (Feast — Ss. Nereus, Achilleus, Pancras) New Advent

(**Mary speaks**) My precious ones, I gave birth to the God-Man through the working of the Holy Spirit, my Heavenly Spouse. I have now been asked again, in this century, to take my children by the hand, through my heart and lead them into the New Advent, the coming of the year 2000 and beyond. This will be a momentous occasion, as many will be drawn again to My Son, the Father and the Holy Spirit, the Most Holy Trinity.

May 13   Refuge

(**Mary speaks**) Please continue to listen, My dear, dear ones. The Sacred Heart of Jesus and My Immaculate Heart are your refuge, your home, your comfort and the place of renewal in times when renewal is needed most. All danger will be overcome, My littlest ones, when you flee to Our Hearts and receive the love and protection waiting for you there. Always seek comfort and refuge in my arms. Know that My Jesus and I long to hold and caress and comfort you always. Love is the answer. The peace of My Son awaits all who come to Him, who come to me.

May 14   (Feast — St. Matthias, Apostle) Imitate Mary

(**Mary speaks**) Dear ones of My Immaculate Heart, I am the Bride of the Holy Spirit, Who guides and challenges all to come to Him now, in all humility, to imitate my virtues of obedience, trust, perseverance, humility, patience and purity. There is not a virtue of mine which you are not being asked to imitate. I am the "Mother of Mercy," Who is Jesus, My Son. Come to me now. I am here to help you, who want to grow in holiness and virtue, imitate me. Many graces and virtues will be yours. As you pray to the Holy Spirit for this, you will begin to walk in the Light of My Son, Jesus.

May 15   (Feast — Ss. Isidore the Farmer & Maria de la Cabeza) Flee to Mary

(**Jesus speaks**) My beloved people, flee to My Mother, dear ones. Escape into her Immaculate Heart. Bring your impatience and thoughts of discouragement and leave them with her, as you hide from the hatred of the world, within the safety of her Mantle. I tell you this because this is the only behavior which brought Me the strength and courage to follow the path and wait for the Day, decreed by My Father, for it to begin.

May 16   Mediatrix of Grace

(**St. Margaret Mary speaks**) Dear sisters and brothers, Please Jesus by pleasing His Mother, the Most Blessed Virgin Mary. She is your greatest ally in coming to know His Heart through Her Heart. Call on the Holy Spirit often, for much needed guidance and direction, along with His Spouse, the ever blessed Holy Mary, Mother of God. She is mother to all of us, who is also our Queen and Mediatrix of all His graces, which He gives Her in abundance to distribute to His children, Her children who ask.

May 17   Immaculate Conception

(**Mary speaks**) Dearest of My Immaculate Heart, it pleases me to be honored and venerated under all titles which have been bestowed upon me. I am your Mother of Mercy, I am the woman of Light, the "Woman Clothed With The Sun." These are some of the titles by which my children honor me. You do well to also honor me under the title found on the "Miraculous Medal" as I am **The Immaculate Conception,** the Immaculate one of God and Mediatrix between My Son Jesus and man.

May 18   (Feast – St. John I, Pope) Direct Channel

(**Mary speaks**) Dear ones, when you bring all to me, there is a direct channel to the Father, through the Son and through My Spouse, the Holy Spirit. When difficulties arise, dear children, call me, call on the Holy Spirit and there will be fountains, rivers of grace, poured into your hearts and souls to help you overcome the obstacles that the evil one is putting there. The adversary cannot survive in a soul, a heart that belongs to me, but he can threaten and make you doubt. Come and pray with me every day for all your needs and for peace.

May 19   Queen of Peace

(**Mary speaks**) My beloved children, I am the Queen of Peace and have come to show my children the way to peace through Him, through His Divine Mercy and His Divine Will. In all my humility and obedience, God the Father accepts my pleas, my prayers, as given to His Son and His Holy Spirit. Do not ever hesitate to follow me. Take my hand. Come with me into the sanctuary of My Immaculate Heart for refuge and comfort. I will show you the peace and glory that awaits you in His Most Divine, Merciful and Loving Sacred Heart.

May 20   (Feast — St. Bernardine of Siena)
Connection Between Man and God

(**Mary speaks**) My precious ones, there is to be for all time the connection between man and God. It is I, the Virgin Mother of the Son. I am the Immaculate One who intercedes for all my children. My children, give all to me. Do all with me, in me, through me, and for me. Come with your joys, sorrows, sadness and your every thought. When you call on me, on Jesus, to take the spirit of the world from you, your life will take on a new dimension of holiness, you have replaced your spirit with Us (Our Spirit).

May 21 Live Total Consecration

(**Mary speaks**) My loved children, The Father, through His Son, My Son, has given me graces to dispense as I will and to whom I will. Those who have been consecrated to me will always have a safe harbor in my heart and will be in communion with Jesus and in His Sacred Heart and His Will. As you live your total consecration to Jesus, through me, every day, you then do all in Him, through Him, with Him and for Him. There should never be a doubt in your minds about this.

May 22 Come to Know Heart of Jesus

(**Jesus speaks**) My dear ones, only those who come to know My Mother will truly come to know Me. It is My wish that you remain near to her, learning from her and allowing her to bring you to My Sacred and Merciful Heart. She is your mother and she is My Mother. She is here for all to come and enjoy her tenderness and her mercy. Come often to her and honor her, as you then crown her with your love and prayers. All Heaven rejoices when they see her being honored. She leads many souls to Me, including those who are in Purgatory.

May 23 Learn From Mary

(**Jesus speaks**) Children of My Sacred Heart, remember how Mary, My most beloved Mother, from her earliest childhood pondered things in her heart? Learn from her. She has much to give you from Me, from the Father and the Holy

Spirit. She is Queen of Heaven and earth and your hearts. She is closely aligned with Our Spirit and it is as We were one. The Holy Trinity has bestowed this honor and grace on her from the beginning of time. We are one with her heart. Where she is, We are. Never doubt this. In her you have the master teacher, especially in the virtues; Our virtues. Listen to her as she leads you to Me and to your eternal happiness and peace.

May 24   Hold Mary's Hand

(**Jesus speaks**) Beloved children, My Virgin Mother, Mary is grace. She is love. She is all you need as a guiding light to Me, with Her Spouse, the Holy Spirit. Do not let go of her hand or be out of her reach and sight, ever. When you do things with Mary, in Mary and through Mary, you are doing them with Me and in so doing, you are glorifying the Father by all that you think, say and do, in My Name. Praise the Father always, giving Him your hearts.

May 25   (Feast — Ss. Bede, Gregory VII, Mary Magdalene de Pazzi) The Treasure

(**Jesus speaks**) When one thanks Me for Mary, dearest children, it is as it should be and as all our children should do. **She is a treasure.** She is a gift of undying value which has been given to all My children. She is all beauty. She is the splendor of the Angels. She is Queen of Heaven and Earth. She is the Jewel in the Crown which lights up the Heavens and the earth, for all to bask in its beauty. She is Mother. She is joy beyond comparison.

May 26   (Feast – St. Philip Neri) Unity of One Body

(**Jesus speaks**) Dearest ones, My Mother is calling you to unity in one Body, under My Headship. My Sacred Heart will reign soon. All Our children must bond together and work together in peace. There must be no division in My ranks. You are all serving the same God. I ask you to please work together as it was always meant to be. It is time to come back and unite under the mantle of My Mother. Convert while you still have time.

May 27   (Feast – St. Augustine of Canterbury, Bishop) Purified Hearts

(**Mary speaks**) My beloved little children, I will never stop interceding at the foot of the Cross for you and yours whom you have given me. Trust me, for I am your mother. Reach out and take my hand more often. I am never far from you. My angels are always with you. No evil can penetrate through your wall of prayer and fasting. With a clean and purified heart, come to me, so I can give your heart, as a great treasure, to My Son, with love.

May 28   Gate to Heart of Jesus

(**Jesus speaks**) Dear ones, when you adore and praise Me through My Mother, you please Me very much. Those who do not honor and love her, cannot love Me. She is the **"Gate into My Heart."** She holds the key. Tell everyone to bring all to My Sacred and Merciful Heart, through My Mother's Immaculate Heart. No one is ever refused when this is done. When They see her, They see Me. I want all to know the intensity of My Love, the way I love each of you, through My Sacred Heart. This can be done through prayer and bringing all to Me, through Mary. This is then a complete Consecration!

May 29   Her Children

(**Jesus speaks**) Children of My Heart, I gave My Mother to all My children from the Cross. You are now all her children as well. Do you realize the precious gift which was given you? She brings all her children to Me, to the Father at all times. She pleads for you and with you, enabling you to see the Holy Spirit working in your lives. She prays that you realize We know your needs for your lives and that your ultimate goal should be the salvation of your souls and to be united with Us for all Eternity in Heaven.

May 30   Mary's Month

(**Mary speaks**) My dearest children, through the years the Father has sent me to our children, all over the world, to bring them to Him, through My Immaculate Heart. Children, can you imagine how your Immaculate Mother feels when she is turned away from a heart, from one of her children's hearts. This is My month. I am holding all of you, my dearest ones, My children, within My Heart. My prayers never cease for you. Won't you please join me, you my loved ones, in these prayers? As you unite your prayers with Mine, your hearts will be with my heart, for the salvation of all souls.

May 31   (Feast – Visitation of Virgin Mary to
St. Elizabeth) Mary's Love

(**Jesus speaks**) My children, your mother, and Mine, Mary, loves you with a love that is not comprehensible. She loves with My Love. Our Hearts beat as One. There is nothing I refuse My Mother when she brings it to Me. She brings all your needs, your weaknesses, your faults to Me. She does not judge. She loves and helps each of you on that path to holiness, to Heaven. She is the perfect model of how one dies to oneself. Follow her example. Pattern your lives after her. The Holy Spirit wants to give you this grace. Please accept it because it is yours for the asking. It is a treasure untold.

Return Love to *"Love"*

JUNE

The Most Holy Trinity
Focus: God the Son

"I Myself am the bread of life. No one who comes to Me shall ever be hungry, no one who believes in Me shall ever thirst. But as I told you, though you have seen Me, you still do not believe. All that the Father gives Me shall come to Me; no one who comes will I ever reject, because it is not to do My own will that I have come down from heaven, but to do the will of Him Who sent Me. It is the will of Him Who sent Me that I should lose nothing of what He has given Me; rather, that I should raise it up on the last day. Indeed, this is the will of My Father, that everyone who looks upon the Son and believes in Him shall have eternal life. Him I will raise up on the last day." (John 6:35-40)

We are not to concern ourselves with anything except that which pleases Him, asking Him at all times to do with us as pleases Him only. It is said that when we become preoccupied with self, He will cease to take care of us, because we then are not doing as He wishes and desires; His Will in us. His Will has to have absolute freedom within us to act as He wishes. It is also said that He will then love Himself with His own love, in us and for us. Our hope must grow in strength and increase our faith and trust in Jesus.

One thing to remember, always, is Jesus, in union with the Holy Trinity, will never change. They cannot. Jesus cannot since HE IS and always WILL BE love, truth, peace, joy, hope for all time and in eternity. We will change, because our God loves us so much. He will have us change so we can come back to Him. Jesus has said: "Do you realize that what the world has to offer is but illusion? Do you not realize that what the Father has to offer, in all reality, is the only means by which you can gain happiness and peace? Why do you continue to look in the wrong places and in the wrong directions? Why do you refuse to accept Me into your lives? I AM HERE! I am in your Tabernacles and in the Communion you receive." He pleads, "please come to Me, now…"

Reflection for the Month

Jesus wants us to ponder these words of His: "*Scripture has it, 'the man without love (unconditional love) has known nothing of God, does not know Me, for God is Love.' As the Father and the Spirit and I are One, We are Love manifested in each other, as We bestow this love to all of Our children. Through Me My children should have come to know this love of God, because the Father sent Me among you at My First Coming. I dwelt with you! I took on flesh and a human nature! I became one like you, in all things, except sin!*

"As Scripture further states, 'Love then consists in this: not that you have loved God, but that He has loved you.' We love as not one of you can imagine, because Our love is Divine. But the Father wanted to show this love to His children, who have never really understood what love was. So, He sent Me, His only Son, as an offering for your sins. If God can and did do this for you, can you not do this for one another and for Him? Remember, God is Love and anyone who abides in love abides in God and God in him and that is the way to bring love to perfection, all through Me."

Prayer

I adore Thee and love Thee, O Divine and Merciful Heart of Jesus, You Who live in the heart of Mary: I beseech you to please come and live and reign in my heart, (here I put in the particular names of those I wish Him to come to in a special way) **and in all hearts, and to perfect in me and each of them and in all people, your pure love.** (this was taken and added to-amended from St. Margaret Mary's prayer)

Resolution

I should look to God, to Jesus, as in myself, no matter in what manner I meditate upon Him, so as to become accustomed to having Him dwell with us and His Divine Presence within me ... within my soul. If I keep my soul, my heart focused on Him I cannot be distracted by anything in or from the world. In the fullness of the love which the Most Holy Trinity will give can be found untold treasures and the grace I will need to accomplish the salvation of my soul.

Meditation for June

Focus: God the Son

**"It is in Christ and through His Blood that we
have been redeemed and our sins forgiven, so
immeasurably generous is God's favor to us.
God has given us the wisdom to understand
fully the mystery, the plan He was pleased to
decree in Christ, to be carried out in the fullness of time: namely, to bring all things in the
heaven's and on earth into one under Christ's
headship."** (Ephesians 1: 7-10)

June 1 (Feast – St. Justin) Way of an Instrument

(**Jesus speaks**) My little ones, you who wish to be My
chosen, will be My vessels, My instruments. You will be used
and filled in different ways for the coming of the Kingdom.
You are to help Me in the task of saving souls. I suggest you
now come before Me, every day, for a least one hour, a **holy
hour**. A visit to Me in the Blessed Sacrament means to be
refreshed, to be renewed, to receive My peace and the graces
necessary to carry on your vital mission, according to the
plan of the Heavenly Father.

June 2 (Feast — Ss. Peter & Marcellinus)
To be Refreshed

(**Jesus speaks**) My dear ones, when you are weary, seek
rest in My Sacred Heart. When you are lonely, seek comfort

in My arms. When you feel empty, take courage and be filled by My Presence in the Blessed Sacrament. When all looks bleak and overwhelming, come to My Mother and to Me and We will refresh you with Our words for your understanding. To understand a mystery more fully, one needs to enter into it more fully. Therefore, the more you are united to Me, the more fully you have surrendered yourself to Me, the more you will know who I am and understand how things happen in our relationship.

June 3   (Feast — St.Charles Lwanga and Companions)
Be Completely One With Jesus

(**Jesus speaks**) My precious children, come often to Me in the Eucharist, in the company of My Sacred Heart in the Blessed Sacrament. There is no better way to gain the union of Our Will that I am offering you. In doing so, there is nothing you will miss, nothing you will be avoiding, nothing that you cannot do without. The outcome of your endeavors will depend on the degree of this unity with Me. Take advantage of Me. Take My strength and gifts to use as your own. Take the power of the Trinity which is possible to those who dwell within Our Oneness. Surrender more to Me. Call on Me to be your all in all. Pray for My Father's Will to be done and then thank and praise.

June 4   Allow Him Into Your Heart

(**St. Margaret Mary speaks**) My dear sisters and brothers in His Sacred and Merciful Heart, our Jesus calls more to devotion to His Sacred Heart. When you open your hearts to receive Him, He grants your heart greater understanding of what His Heart is giving and what His Heart wishes in return from you. You are then given His strength and courage and much perseverance, obedience and patience, which flood into your hearts from His Heart. When you allow Him to venture into your heart from His Heart, as you listen and begin to know, in the silence of your heart, to recognize Him, when He knocks and seeks you out, He then sees what you are lacking and He fills you with Himself.

June 5   (Feast — St. Boniface, Bishop)
Desire to Please Him

(**St. Margaret Mary speaks**) Dear brothers and sisters, Jesus wishes to have your heart for His very own. Learn to be one with Him, with the Most Holy Trinity. Always seek Him out. Always accept what He desires of you, willingly and with a complete desire on your part of pleasing Him and Him alone. Let Him do with you as He Wills. Allow your heart to accept anything which will give pleasure to His Divine Heart, Who wishes to be with each heart, always. Jesus revealed to me, as I read in His Heart the following words: *"My Love reigns in suffering. It triumphs in humility and It rejoices in unity."*

June 6   (Feast — St. Norbert, Bishop) Live For Jesus

(**Jesus speaks**) My beloved children, you must live each day for Me, in Me and as I Will for you, giving all to Me, wholly of yourselves. When you come in adoration and much love of Me in the Blessed Sacrament, I see your heart that looks at Me and I return that love in abundance. Continue to focus on Me in this way. If only you realized the benefits from just being with Me, in complete communion of hearts, My Heart with your heart. To do this is to be blest in wonderful ways. This is how you find peace and the balance that is needed in your lives.

June 7   Created to Return Love

(**Jesus speaks**) Little ones of My Heart, there is no offense that will not be forgiven, if you come in true contrition of heart and soul to Us. We love you very much and want for that love to be returned. Some do not believe this, because, as God they feel We do not need anything. This is not true. We do need you. You were created to know, to love and to serve your Creator, your God. I came to earth to show you how this was to be, by My serving you, by My love for each of you. You were created to return the love We give and have for you, to your God; to trust Him in all things and at all times. You have been saved because of My Suffering, Death and Resurrection. I expiated, suffered for all your sins, for all sin since Adam and Eve, until I shall come again, to take all of you, who wish, with Me into Eternal joy and happiness.

June 8   The Walk With Jesus

(**Jesus speaks**) Dearest children, trust Me completely. Come to Me and let Me lead you in faith. Let Me lead you in that walk that I wish each of you to take with Me. It is My Way not yours. But, it is your will to choose which way you wish to go. The way is clearly marked. Both ways are clearly marked. What will be your choice? **Trust and have faith.**

Pray for this grace. It shall be given if you ask. I want the best for you, My beloved children. The best is when you have found Me! Let nothing disturb your peace as anxiety and worry are not from your God. Be assured of the grace to be able to walk with Me, if this be your choice.

June 9 (Feast — St. Ephrem the Syrian, Doctor) Belonging Completely to Jesus

(**Mary speaks**) My beloved children of My Immaculate Heart, when you sincerely and humbly of heart give all to Jesus through me, you then belong completely to Him, through me, the Mother and the Queen of Heaven. When you give of yourself entirely to Jesus and willingly carry your cross after Him all the days of your life, you must renounce the world and all it has to offer. You renounce that "self" that wants to control you. You die to self so His grace can live wholly in you. You then have given Him everything you are, have, think, say and do, to use as He knows is best for you and for your soul and the souls of the many. Dearest ones, you were always meant to be in the Body of Christ and to be Christ-like. It is time to show the world your Christ-like attitudes, by putting on the Mind of Christ, by living and acting out now, as you have been taught, for so many, many years.

June 10 Jesus Gives Completely of Himself

(**Mary speaks**) My children, it is hard to believe, to comprehend the fullness of joy as Jesus gives of Himself wholly and completely to you, as you invite Him to do, through your consecration to Him. Imagine, your God, your Creator, your

Savior giving Himself to you, when you ask. All He desires is that you, in your way, give back to Him, a small measure of yourself to Him, in praise and thanksgiving. He waits, patiently, until you are ready to give Him all of you, without a hesitation of any sort on your part. He then can fashion you as was meant to be from the beginning of time

June 11   (Feast — St. Barnabas, Apostle)
     Allowing Jesus to Work in You

(**Mary speaks**) Little ones of My Immaculate Heart, Jesus loves completely. He gives totally of Himself. All you need do is look at Him on the Cross to see this. When you allow Him to work in you, your understanding will increase as to insights into these mysteries of faith. His Wisdom will permeate your being and instead of wandering around without light, you will be bathed in light, His Light. You will then see as you have never seen before. Come to Him often, so He can work in you. Come to Him in adoration. Come to Him every day at the Holy Sacrifice of the Mass. Let Him feed you with His Heavenly Food, with Himself. You will then want or need anything else, for you will have it all. **You will have Him!** You are then one with Him and He and you are completely one in His love. You have allowed Him to work in you as was always meant to be.

June 12   The Oneness of the Triune God

(**Jesus speaks**) My beloved children, as the Father and the Spirit and I are One, Our love is manifested in Each Other, as We bestow this love to all Our children. Scripture has it that the man without love has known nothing of God, does not know Me, for God is Love. Through Me, the world, My children, should have come to know this love of God, because the Father sent Me among you at My first coming. I dwelt with you! I took on flesh and human nature. I became one like you in all things, except sin. Please know, loved ones, that WE, the Most Holy Trinity, love each of you very much. We are One and We are Love. **I AM LOVE FOR I AM GOD.**

June 13   (Feast — St. Anthony of Padua)
                        Keeping in the Heart of Jesus

(**Jesus speaks**) Dear ones of My Sacred and Merciful Heart, completely abandon all for Me. Always keep focused on Me. Keep within My Heart through My precious jewel, My Mother's Immaculate Heart. Ask My Mother each day how to please her, as there is nothing she does that does not please Us, the Most Holy and Undivided Trinity. If you wish to be in My Will and are striving for this, go to the Immaculate One, as she guides you who wish, to submit all to Me. When your heart is ready to beat in unison with My Heart, you will include Me in ALL of your life; all your thoughts, your hopes and your desires.

June 14   Mirror Jesus — Live Mercy

(**Jesus speaks**) Dearest children of My Heart, when you realize how important it is to rid yourselves of "self," you will strive to do this through prayer. There is too much pride in the world. Too many want to change others but not themselves. As you judge others you cannot see that what you may be judging in others is exactly what you should see in yourself. Take a close look at yourself. The heart is the perfect mirror and this should mirror Me. You need to have My charity and mercy towards others, yourself and towards Me. Live My Mercy in all you do, think and say. Your world needs My mercy as it never has before. My Chaplet of Divine Mercy is a most important prayer, to be prayed for souls and for their conversions. Help Me My children, to let more people know of My mercy and love, so when they see you, your mercy and love, they will see Me. Never cease praying for this.

June 15   Walk the Walk of Jesus

(**Jesus speaks**) Little ones, if you are to have peace in your communities, your countries, within your very selves, you need to rid yourself of all negative attitudes and practices. You need to become that little child I so want you to be. My children, I want you to walk the walk I walk. I want you to Image Me, to image Mary Immaculate. You cannot do this if all you see in the mirror is you: the person you love to believe that is so much better than those around you. Most of you could rid yourselves of so much "junk" if you would only give it all to Me. Then, take up your cross and follow Me. Focus on Me and My Way which is Truth and Light. You who judge or feel superior, who like to hold on to the "Me" attitudes, have less a chance of letting the Holy Spirit work in you. All hearts need healing. There is nothing I cannot heal and want to heal, as long as your will gives Me free rein to work in you.

June 16   Ability to Change

(**Jesus speaks**) My little ones, you will experience trust and My love when you allow Me to be united to your heart, as you accept and do all I tell your heart, as I request of you. Your ability to change, to be one with Me, is a matter of openness to the Gifts I wish to give you. Your strength is built up in the quiet of doing nothing, except that of being with Me. In the quiet of listening, obedience is develped. In the quiet of just being. Love will flood your heart. Wait on My Will for you.

June 17   Your Whole Being

(**Jesus speaks**) My precious children, I need your hearts, your whole beings. I need your prayers, fasting, sacrifices and I need them **NOW**, for yourselves and for all souls. Do not worry or become anxious for what the future may hold for you. **Dwell in Me.** Today is what is important, not tomorrow. Be at peace, My peace. Please strengthen yourselves with prayer and complete trust in Me. There is nothing to fear, little ones, when you are completely Mine. Choose Me, little ones, in all you do and in all you are. Choose the love that no one else can give you. My love is all you will ever need. My love is there for your complete protection and complete fulfillment. My love is there for your every need, your every wish and every desire. Continue to be at peace knowing I am with you.

June 18   The World Needs to See Jesus in You

(**Jesus speaks**) My beloved little ones, more need to see My joy, mercy and love in each of you. All who see you will then see Me. When all realize and comprehend that **I am the Way, The Truth, The Life and Light,** you will then rejoice, as you will know a happiness you have never had before. You and the world, cannot do without this, without Me. Nothing is as important as the time spent with Me and My desires for you. Children, it is important that each of you continue to ask Me to cleanse your hearts, to heal them and to create new hearts in you. Ask for your heart to resemble My Heart. In this way Satan cannot penetrate your souls. Your heart then belongs to Me. Please do not take your heart back from Me once given, as I have not finished fashioning it as I would like.

June 19   Learn from Jesus

(**Jesus speaks**) Loved ones, learn My Virtues. Through humility and charity you will find a sure path to Me, to dying to one's self, to abandoning all to Me and to giving up your will in favor of My Will. Learn to conform yourself to My virtues of humility, charity and love when you deal with others. You must love all in mercy. When you look at someone, look with the light of love, which is charity and mercy. When you look into the face of a brother or sister, you are looking at Me. **If you cannot see Me in them, you have not died to the world, to self.** You have not learned to be "Christ-like" — to be Me.

June 20   Master Builder

(**Jesus speaks**) Dearest ones of My Merciful Heart, all of you, My beloved children, need a master architect and builder. I am that Architect and Builder Who will build a strong faith in your hearts and souls, if you allow Me to do so. The price is high: your souls given to Me in the same trust, love and joy that I give to you. As I build, I also serve. I wish you to do the same. Follow My Path of Light to others. Show others how firm your structure of faith is through the wisdom you have learned from Me.

June 21   (Feast — St. Aloysius Gonzaga)
            Jesus' Divine Mercy

(**Jesus speaks**) My children, there is much I want to say and have said about My Divine Mercy. My beloved Faustina has taken all My Words to her and has passed them on to all of you. I want all to know of this Mercy of Mine and what I have asked for through this devotion and what it is I desire of you. I desire that My Mercy be celebrated in a solemn way, each year, in each of My Churches throughout the world, on the second Sunday of Easter. This is to be known as the Feast of Divine Mercy. My priests and the pastors of My flocks should be teaching My sheep, all the souls under their care, all through the year, how to live in Mercy, as I have given to My daughter Faustina, as well as to My beloved Margaret Mary before her. My priest sons need to live in My Light, Love, Peace and Mercy. This is so important and should be done all through the year.

June 22   (Ss. John Fisher & Thomas More)
            Adornment for Souls

(**Mary speaks**) Beloved children, the love which My Jesus has for each of you is an adornment for your souls. The light of My Son will shine forth as a beacon to light the Way for you who seek Him as a refuge. The love and grace of My Jesus never stops overflowing onto all those who seek this grace and love and then receive it gladly with an eager heart.

June 23   Be Not Afraid

(**Jesus speaks**) My beloved little ones, how I love you! I beg you, no matter what may be going on around you, **be not afraid.** Keep Me in your heart and close to your every move and breath. Keep focused on what is good and what is love and mercy and not on what the world would have you focused on. My peace I instill and infuse within your hearts and all hearts who follow My Light and My Truth. Let faith rule your very beings. Do not ever fear for I am with You at all times. Call on Me and I will be there. Let hope and joy permeate your very beings and you will know My Presence. Put Me back in your lives, in your hearts, for this is where I belong. Please pray for those who have become so tepid and lukewarm. Those who have put Me first in your lives, please pray for your wayward brothers and sisters. Come back to Me. Adore Me. Praise Me. Pray with Me and to Me. Love Me. I love you.

June 24   (Feast – Birth of St. John the Baptist)
           Miracles Happen

(**Jesus speaks**) Children of My Heart, those of you who invite Me into your lives, into your hearts, I can then, in turn, heal and give you grace which is needed for you to be able to give Me your hearts and your will. This then enables a transformation to take place in you. Miracles happen daily for those who wish this. I speak to all who wish to listen and to be led by Me. I come to you through My Word, through My Church and through My Teachings. I wish to give each of you the grace to be able to decide in your free will to come and follow Me, NOW, TODAY. Indecision should no longer be a part of your life.

June 25   Praying for Loved Ones

(**Jesus speaks**) Dear ones, once you have given someone you are praying for to Me, to Mary Immaculate, through your total consecration of them, to Our Hearts, there is no more to be concerned about. They then belong wholly and fully to Us: even if they know this not, nor acknowledge this in their own lives. They are Ours, as all of you are, who have come to Us with your hearts and souls in your hands, in total Trust, giving all to Us, in love and mercy, for yourselves, for them and for Me.

June 26   Pattern Your Families After Holy Family

(**Jesus speaks**) Beloved little ones, I have come to help sanctify and elevate the family to the status of My Holy Family (when I came to earth). I came to teach families to model their lives after Ours: to pray together, to have God the center of all they do. When this happens again, peace will be restored and the Reign of My Sacred Heart, along with the Immaculate Heart of My Mother, will smile on each of Our children. Your consecration of yourselves and your families will herald in this Reign of My Sacred Heart. It is now time to stop doing the things that take you and your families away from Me.

June 27 (Feast — Our Lady of Perpetual Help) Seeds of Grace

(**Jesus speaks**) My children, come to Me to be filled. Help Me fill each vessel that comes. I will do the rest. I plant the seeds through you and then, as doors open, My grace and mercy can penetrate through hearts and souls. Nothing is impossible for Me for I alone am God. Put yourselves completely in My Hands and Heart, My dear ones, in complete faith and trust, each day. You will then see many transformations take place. There will be many miracles as I will be the Center of all you do and all you are. Do this only one day at a time, each day.

June 28 (Feast — St. Iraneus, Bishop) Commitment to Prayer

(**Jesus speaks**) Beloved ones of My Sacred Heart, when you see harm being done, a wrong being created, atrocities committed, pray immediately, in unison with Us, for that person or persons and then see how changes will occur. Yes, even your bad laws can be changed in this manner. It costs you nothing, except your commitment to pray. The cost of this commitment is time. Who has given you this time? Will you and are you, willing to give back some of that time, now, to help save your families, your country and your world? Can you spend AN HOUR A DAY WITH ME, in the silence of your hearts, in front of Me, with Me, as you and I pray in reparation for the sins of the world? Will you try?

June 29 (Feast – Ss. Peter and Paul)
Living Eternity on Earth

(**Jesus speaks**) Dearest children, you must remember that real life is living a portion of Eternity in the here and now. When you permit Me to be wholly and completely a part of you, in you, with you in Me, you begin to realize what it will be like to live a life with Us for all of Eternity. Living that does not include Us is immature and empty, devoid of the reality of why man was created. When I am allowed to live in you, act in and for you as I know you need, when you no longer resist My Will and have given Me the freedom to work in and with you, then marvelous and miraculous things happen.

June 30 Truth and Love

(**Jesus speaks**) Beloved and most precious children; My words are Truth. My words do not need explanation. I explain to each heart, when asked, and when a heart is looking for the truth. I desire your souls and your hearts to reflect on Me, to hear Me, to listen to My Truth and then reflect on what I am telling your hearts of My Truth. You are not to draw on what you think is truth, only what Is Truth. Contrary to popular belief, your God needs you very much. This is not a need as you experience, but one which you will understand when you are in eternity with Us. God is Love and anyone who abides in love, abides in God and God in him and that is the way to bring love to perfection. Let Me lead you in faith. Come to Me. Trust Me. Let Me lead you in that walk I wish each of you to take, with Me. It is My Way, not yours. But, it is your will to choose which way you wish to go. The way is clearly marked. Both ways are clearly marked. WHAT WILL BE YOUR CHOICE?

JULY

The Most Holy Trinity
Focus: God The Holy Spirit
and Defend the Faith

"God has not called us to immorality but to holiness: hence, whoever rejects these instructions, rejects not man, but God who sent His Holy Spirit upon you." (1 Thessalonians 4:7-8)

This month we focus on the Holy Spirit, the Third Person of the Most Holy Trinity. Jesus has said to continue to open our hearts and minds to what the Holy Spirit wants to do within our person, what He wants to speak to us and to enlighten us. Jesus has said that through the Holy Spirit we come to know our God, the Father and the Son in a personal way. We learn how much They love us, unconditionally, no matter what we may think and no matter what the world is telling us. They, through the working of Their Holy Spirit, are with us NOW and will be for all of eternity.

As we allow the eyes of our hearts and minds to be opened, we will be transformed by this same Holy Spirit Who worked wonders on that first Pentecost day. We will find we have a deep hunger and a willingness to accept Jesus and His Love more completely in our lives. Through the Holy Spirit and through our saying "yes" to His working within us, as Mary did so many years ago, we will find we will gradually put on the Mind and Heart of Christ; we will become more Christlike, as was always intended. We then become those children of His who are the meek and humble of heart, those who will inherit the Kingdom. Our names will truly be written in Heaven.

The Holy Spirit has this to say: *"I dwell in hearts and souls who wish My Light and the grace of My gifts, which I want to give in much abundance. I am Strength and Courage and want to give this to you, to help you in your walk to holiness. Once a heart, a soul, has given itself to Me to help, to guide, to direct, to counsel, to do as We, the Triune Godhead Wills for it, there is nothing that the soul then cannot attain in the realm of the Kingdom, here and later on in Heaven."*

Reflection for the Month

We need to run to our mother, the Virgin Mother of Jesus and the Spouse of the Holy Spirit. to receive her from Jesus as He gave her to us from the Cross. When we choose Mary as our mother, we are choosing Her Son, Jesus, the Father in Heaven who chose her from the beginning of time and we choose the Holy Spirit, her Spouse.

The only way to make true spiritual progress, to mature in your spiritual life, is to call on the Holy Spirit for everything. When you have Him, you have it all: you have God the Father, God the Son, and the Mother of the Son, the favored daughter of the Father and the Spouse of Their Holy Spirit. There is nothing more to ask for or to need. The soul who has the Holy Spirit and allows Him to work in it completely, surrendering all to Him, has a taste of Heaven here on earth. The Holy Spirit is the dynamic we need to catapult us to holiness, to sainthood. It is through His working in us and with us and through us that we achieve the graces and gifts we will need to face our every day trials and duties, according to how He wishes to work His Will in us. All of this cannot happen without our permission; allowing Him to work in us. This is a gift of great value, one to be treasured. When the soul has realized that without the working of the Holy Spirit in it, it is nowhere, it is only then that, giving our free will to Him, He can work miracles and transform us into the spiritual person we were always meant to be.

Prayer

Dearest Holy One of God the Father and of Jesus, our brother and Savior, You truly are the Soul of my soul. I adore you, I praise you, I thank you for all you are doing in my life. I love you. Please come into my heart and soul now to guide, direct, instruct, admonish, console, enlighten as You Will. Bring me all of your Gifts and the virtues that come from these gifts that I may imitate Jesus and Mary more fully this day and those virtues that will help me overcome my faults, so as not to offend you by sin. Tell me what it is You wish of me this day and then command me to do it, for it is Your Will I desire and not mine. Amen.

Resolution

I want to become another Christ. I want to become Eucharist. I want you, dearest Holy Spirit of the Father and the Son, to work in me as You know is best for me, at any given moment. Please give me the grace to always listen so I can hear your voice. Dwell within me as I know I am your Temple and want what it is you want for me at every moment of my life.

Meditations For July

Focus: God the Holy Spirit and Defend the Faith

> "But they rebelled, and grieved His Holy Spirit; so He turned against them like an enemy and fought against them. Then they remembered the days of old and Moses, His servant; where is he who brought up out of the sea the shepherd of His flock? Where is he who put His Holy Spirit in their midst...?" (Isaiah 63:10-11)

July 1 (Feast — Bl. Juniper Serra) Unshakable Faith

(**Jesus speaks**) My beloved children, you are My chosen beacons of light for a darkening world. You must always have absolute, unshakable confidence and faith in Me, in My Mother and in what My Holy Spirit will inspire. You then should follow these inspirations from the Holy Spirit blindly, even though at times it might not make sense to you. Everyone who follows Me, through the working of the Holy Spirit, and who listen to Him in trust and in faith, are His chosen ones. Through the working of this same Holy Spirit He will encourage, enlighten you in strength and guide your hearts.

July 2 Listen Carefully

(**Mary speaks**) My dearest children, keep in prayer with me at all times. I love you with my mother's heart. I will fill you with the necessary peace and love you will need now and in the days to come. Listen carefully to the Holy Spirit, as He will be guiding you and yours along the way of holiness for you and all who choose to join with Him, in the work He has outlined for each of you Will you help in bringing more souls to Us, as My Spouse the Holy Spirit will inspire? You may be called, my children, to arise at any hour, when you are beckoned by me, from Jesus to follow what the sweet, gentle voice of the Holy Spirit calls you to. Continue to pray for wisdom and understanding from the Holy Spirit. He will instruct you as He knows what you need.

July 3   (Feast – St. Thomas, Apostle)
           Go Forward in Love

(**Jesus speaks**) Dear ones, as you go forward in love each day, keep the Holy Spirit close to your hearts with your constant prayer of consecration to Him, to My Sacred Heart and to the Immaculate Heart of Mary. There will be a special anointing now from the Holy Spirit, to your hearts and minds and many graces and gifts will be given you, if you ask. He wants to bestow on you a continuous stream of gifts, fruits and virtues. As you receive the gifts He gives, you will increase in virtue and the fruits will be evident.

July 4   (Our Lady of Refuge of Sinners)
           Listen in Silence and in Prayer

(**Mary speaks**) My dearest children, the Holy Spirit comes to those who keep their hearts open, trouble free, with no thoughts or desires beyond what He wishes to give. Do not get too busy with things of the world. Stay in quiet with me and with My Son, so you will be able to recognize the voice of the Holy Spirit and receive the gifts He wants to give you.

You need to pray continuously in your heart, for the grace of His gifts which He has to give, as well as the direction and guidance for your life. Children, it is important you pray and work closely with the Holy Spirit. His gifts will prove invaluable to your soul.

July 5 (Feast – St. Anthony Zaccaria)
Heed What He Says

(**Mary speaks**) Beloved little ones, it is important for you to listen in order to hear the Holy Spirit. Listen in the silence of your hearts and in prayer and then do what is being asked of you, by Him. The Holy Spirit will continue to speak to a heart which is open to hearing Him. Carefully heed what He tells you. Rely on your Angels to direct you on the path to find Him (the Holy Spirit). Pray with them and to them. Talk to them. Keep close to me and to the Holy Spirit for continued guidance and direction. This is important, as Satan is ready to deceive you in many ways. We are here to help.

July 6 (Feast – St. Maria Goretti) Progress in Prayer

(**Mary speaks**) My loved little children, praise to the Father, the Son and the Holy Spirit. As you progress in prayer, invoke the Holy Spirit to be with you. He will dwell in special ways in each heart and will give you guidance and direction on your path to holiness. Ask the Holy Spirit each day in prayer for His discernment, His enlightenment, His grace for the virtues you need for strength and courage to be able to persevere in humility, obedience, charity and love. Be open, in complete trust, to all the graces that will be given each of you, according to your needs, as God sees it. Call on and depend on the Holy Spirit, for all your guidance and direction.

July 7   Led by the Holy Spirit

(**Jesus speaks**) My beloved children, I urge you to listen at all times to what I speak to your heart, through the Holy Spirit. We speak to all who listen and wish to be led by Us. You are to be grounded in a strong, unshakable faith and trust in Me, in My Word, in My loved son, your Pope and what he teaches and in My Church, through opening your hearts to hear the Holy Spirit. He will bring you closer and closer and closer to Me, to the Truth.

July 8   Gifts

(**Mary speaks**) Loved ones of My Immaculate Heart, the Holy Spirit is a gift. He has many gifts to bestow on hearts and souls. Please, my little ones, never refuse these gifts from the Holy Spirit, for no one can survive without them. Much grace and mercy abound and are bestowed on you who accept these gifts. I urge you to take all the gifts given you, listen to the Holy Spirit for guidance on how to use these gifts and then use them wisely. When your faith is weak, pray to the Holy Spirit to strengthen this faith and then trust, live in hope and practice the faith He gives you.

July 9   Ask for Grace

(**Mary speaks**) Beloved children of Mine, when you ask the Holy Spirit for direction and His Wisdom to know what is truth and what is not, He will gladly give you this grace. The Holy Spirit wants to give much grace to all Our children. You will know when you are being given grace and then you can either accept it or not. Dear ones, ask for the graces that are there for you. This is essential to your spiritual health. Do not be concerned about your bodily health over your spiritual health. When you are spiritually alive with the Holy Spirit being allowed to work in you, you know We will also take care of the body's welfare, according to His plan for you.

July 10   All Gifts and Graces Given

(**Jesus speaks**) My dear children, Our Holy Spirit is prepared to gift you with all the gifts and graces you will ever need. He will shower you in abundance. All that needs doing is to ask for ALL of them (His gifts) and He will give you what He knows you need and what He wishes to bestow in your soul. He will also let you know what needs working on and then you are to work on it. Listen to Him. Pray to Him. There has never been a greater need in the hearts of man, as there is now, for the Holy Spirit to work in each of you. Let Him consume you. Let Him guide and direct you in everything.

July 11   (Feast – St. Benedict, Abbot)
Meditate on Scripture

(**Jesus speaks**) My precious children, read the Holy Words of Scripture every day. As I feed you through this, meditate on The Word. Ask Our Holy Spirit to enlighten you as to the meaning of what is said to you through the Scriptures. Give all, including your distractions, to the Holy Spirit and He will give you an abundance of grace, understanding, wisdom, and discernment. He will enlighten your mind and your heart as to what The Word is saying just for you.

July 12   Open Your Heart

(**Mary speaks**) My loved ones, I wish you now to read from Holy Scripture, 1 John 4:16-19. Please pray about these words and their meaning for you. These words have been inspired by the Holy Spirit. Ask Him to open your heart to what these words will mean to you and for you. These words have to do with fear. You must know any and all fear (except for a holy fear of the Lord) is not from God. Only love is from God through the Holy Spirit's inspiration.

July 13   Holy Spirit's Direction

(**Jesus speaks**) My children, seek the gifts of understanding and wisdom of My Holy Spirit. Do not be fooled by your own understanding of these. Sit before Me in silence and ask for these gifts from the Holy Spirit, if you would truly know Who I am. Allow My Spirit to direct you more completely, more fully in all things. Practice this, My children, for it is a knowledge you will always need.

July 14   (Feast – Blessed Kateri Tekawitha)
                The Tiny Whisper

(**St. Teresa of Avila speaks**) My dear brothers and sisters in Christ, please listen with all your hearts to the voice of the Spirit Who comes as a tiny whisper in a heart. He comes like a whisper so that all of God's children will strain to hear His

Will. It is this kind of listening and attention that trains us in obedience and prepares us to fight against our inclination to laziness and self-deception. Listen and pay attention so you won't miss a word He speaks to you.

July 15   (Feast – St. Bonaventure) Pray on the Hour

(**Mary speaks**) My beautiful children, pray to the Holy Spirit each day, on the hour if necessary, for His enlightenment, His discernment, His grace for the virtues you will need. Pray to Him for strength and courage and to strengthen your faith and trust. It is important you pray and work closely with the Holy Spirit. His gifts will prove invaluable to your soul. The Holy Spirit works in wonderful, mysterious and wise ways and only the heart and soul, who is in communion with Us, in silence and in peace, will be able to hear Him. He wishes to give in abundance the virtues you ask for. He will answer according to what He knows is your need, at a given time.

July 16   (Our Lady of Mt. Carmel) Gifts and Fruits

(**Jesus speaks**) Beloved children, listen to the Holy Spirit, Who will descend on you as He did at the first Pentecost. You will then receive His gifts. Some will be different from others, but I tell you My children, ask for all of them and their fruits, which are the virtues. You will know the gifts, graces and virtues that are coming to you, as you live your lives with the Holy Spirit and with My Holy Mother, the Spouse of the Holy Spirit. I beseech you not to hesitate in accepting any grace, gift or virtue from the Holy Spirit that will strengthen your hearts and your wills to be Mine

July 17   Closer Each Day

(**Jesus speaks**) Dearest ones, you My children, are Temples of the Holy Spirit. Bring Him closer to you each day as He inspires you and then do as He inspires. Listen carefully in the quiet and in the stillness of your hearts. Otherwise you may miss your opportunity that could be of great and grave importance to you. The Spirit of Wisdom and Truth will come to your aid every time you call upon Him. You may believe this and count on His help completely. He will not let you down, I promise you. It is His Nature to be Wisdom and Light to all who call upon His help.

July 18   Shield of Protection

(**Mary speaks**) My dear ones, continue to always listen to the voice of My Beloved Spouse. His Wisdom is all you will need as a shield of protection with which to defend all you believe and know to be true. The truth is the ultimate weapon of defense against all the powers of hell. This truth is gotten from The Holy Spirit by Divine inspiration. When you listen to the Holy Spirit's directions and my prompting, there will be much that can be done for souls. We want all souls. Will you help us?

July 19   Judging and Criticizing

(**Holy Spirit speaks**) Dear ones, Our children must put a stop to all judging and criticizing. With My grace this is possible. Without it, it will not be possible. Judging belongs only to God. You must **never** criticize a priest. This is most serious. Being critical and judgmental goes against the virtue of Charity and leads you away from loving unconditionally. It will lead you to sins of pride if not overcome. Do not allow this. We cannot (the Holy Trinity) abide in a soul who judges. This sin in itself could keep a soul from coming into its glory in Heaven. It would warrant a long stay in Purgatory.

July 20   Seek Forgiveness

(**Holy Spirit speaks**) My children, children of the Triune Godhead, avoid judging (wrongfully) each other, yourselves, or your God, as this will lead to resentments. Seek forgiveness immediately. If you have harmed someone by these resentments, judgments or criticisms, you must ask that person for forgiveness. You should, in turn, forgive anyone who has judged you or has talked about you. Being hurtful, judgmental, or critical in thoughts is just as bad. What you should do when this type of sin occurs is to immediately go into silent prayer, calling on Me for help, then leave the judging up to God, Who knows hearts and motivations.

July 21   Self-Centerdness and Anger

(**Holy Spirit speaks**) Little ones, selfishness and being self-centered are the cause of anger. This then causes you to demand too much of others and of yourself. This all feeds on ego. My children, We know your weaknesses, your vulnerabilities, your sinfulness, but so does Satan. He will try to deceive you, to convince you of the opposite of what We will be telling you, or inspiring you, for your own good. When you call on Us, We will provide you the necessary grace you will need to do battle against this evil one.

July 22   (Feast — St. Mary Magdalen)
Perfect as the Heavenly Father is Perfect

(**Jesus speaks**) My children, there are many souls who cannot come to join Us immediately in Heaven upon their departure from your world, because to be with Us for all Eternity in Our Presence, there must not be the slightest stain of any kind or nature of sin, to impede the soul from being in full communion with the saints and angels in heaven. You cannot come to Us in Heaven unless you are truly "perfect as My Heavenly Father is perfect." This is how you were created and how He intended you, His children, to be, enabling you to be in Him and see Him, in His true and magnificent Majesty, His true Presence. Our Holy Spirit works in souls to help them realize their sinfulness and how We see you and then gives you, by His grace, the opportunity of repentance. Call on Him often to convict you of your faults and what it should be you are to confess.

July 23   (Feast — St. Bridget of Sweden)
Working of the Holy Spirit

(**Jesus speaks**) Dear children, please give Me your hearts, your souls and your wills. I cannot take them unless you willingly give them NOW to Me. When I have you completely and we are truly one in the Spirit, and through the working of the Holy Spirit in your beings, miracles will happen. Peace, love and happiness will live in each of you and I will reign in all hearts, as was meant to be, from the beginning of time. The Holy Spirit will pour into your soul, His courage and strength, with the perseverance to be able to overcome all obstacles that are put in your way. The Holy Spirit, when asked, will direct, guide and enlighten your mind as to the sins on your soul at any one time.

July 24   Seek Guidance

(**Jesus speaks**) Dear little ones, always ask for the guidance and direction of Our Holy Spirit in all you do. Seek this guidance in the small as well as the momentous decisions about choices you are to make. Ask your beloved Mother, the Immaculate Virgin Mary, to hold your hand and guide you to her Spouse, the Holy Spirit, Who will take you and lead you to the eternal splendor of what the Father has planned. TRUST AND HAVE FAITH. Pray for this grace from the Holy Spirit. It shall be given you, if you ask.

July 25   (Feast — St James, Apostle)
Your Faith — a Priceless Jewel

(**Jesus speaks**) Beloved children, never hesitate to defend your faith which I have given you. It is a priceless jewel and should be cared for as such. Your reward in heaven will be great. Know that I am always there with those who defend My Church, as is Our Holy Spirit. You will have much support from heaven as well. Our Holy Spirit will inspire you beyond your capacities to understand when you defend the Faith of your Father. It will even be hard for you to believe what is being said by you, when you are saying it.

Know then it is indeed the Holy Spirit at work within you. Thank you my loved ones, who defend Me, My vicar on earth and My Church.

July 26 (Feast — St. Anne & St. Joachim)
Stand up For the Truth

(**Jesus speaks**) Dear ones, do not hesitate to gently but firmly stand up for the Truth, to stand up for Me. Do as I would do in any one given situation. Always ask yourself is this how Jesus would do it? Then call on the Holy Spirit for His enlightenment and direction in all you think, say and do, at all times. Remember, the evil one can put words and thoughts in your minds. Always rebuke him and call on My Precious Blood to know it is from Me, from Our Holy Spirit. You are apostles and disciples of Mine. With this comes the responsibility to defend Me, to defend My Church and My Vicar (the Pope), when the situation arises that needs defending. The Holy Spirit will always be there to help with the words, the thoughts, and the way something should be done.

July 27 Your Reward

(**Jesus speaks**) My beloved children, for those of you who defend Our Faith, your reward in Heaven will be great. Know too, that I am always there with those who defend My Church. When words drastically change My Holy Sacrifice, it should be noticed by all of you. It pleases Me there are many astute listeners. There is no need to worry about theology or what you may or may not know. Put it in His Hands and let Him work within you.

July 28 Renewing the Earth

(**Mary speaks**) Children of My Immaculate Heart, the Holy Spirit of the Father and the Son is renewing and revitalizing much of the earth now and there will be seen many more conversions. A great multitude are coming back to Him, Who is your Creator, as He always had planned. Through the Holy Spirit, there is beginning to be a great spiritual awareness in My children's lives. Your quest for holiness will be in your grasp, if you remain in communion with Us.

July 29 (Feast – St. Martha) Call on the Holy Spirit

(**Jesus speaks**) My loved children, my wish is that all of you, my loved ones, persevere at all times and call on the Holy Spirit for the grace you will need in this and in all else that is needed. He knows when you need something and how to help you best, as long as you are open to Him, to being purified, to being corrected and are open to change. When you have let go of self and are no longer holding feelings of resentment or anger, you are learning to be meek, humble and gentle as I am. You are then being submissive to Me, to My Love and to My Mercy. The Holy Spirit gives much grace to a soul who learns this lesson.

July 30 (Feast – St. Peter Chrysologus, Bishop/Doctor) No Longer an Option

(**Mary speaks**) My loved little ones, you who come to pray with me in front of the Blessed Sacrament, many graces and blessings are given you. To pray like this **is no longer an**

option. Pray to the Holy Spirit to open up time for you, when you feel there is no available time, so you then can spend more time in complete union with Our Hearts. So much can be accomplished by this small effort on your part, dearest ones. Praying like this is an extension of the Mass and most important. When you spend time with Us in front of the Blessed Sacrament, you receive many blessings not only for yourself, but for the many souls who will benefit from it, as you unite and give each visit to His Sacred Heart, through My Immaculate Heart, all for the honor and glory of God.

July 31   (Feast — St. Ignatius of Loyola)
Strength and Courage

(Holy Spirit speaks) Beloved, I am STRENGTH AND COURAGE and want to give this to you, to help you in your walk to holiness. There is nothing that should be uppermost in your mind than to strive for the gifts which I will give when you will need them. I know when it is time and when a soul is ready to receive a grace, a gift, and it is then there for the asking. Unless you ask, it goes unused within you. You are to continue unceasingly to pray for grace, sanctifying grace.

AUGUST

The Most Holy Trinity
Focus: God the Father

"(Eternal life is this: to know You, the only true God, and Him Whom You have sent, Jesus Christ.) I have given You glory on earth by finishing the work You gave Me to do. Do You now, Father, give Me glory at your side, a glory I had with you before the world began." (John 17:3-6)

God the Father has an eternal plan for our salvation. He saved us and called us to a holy life, not according to our works, but according to His own design and the grace bestowed on us in Christ Jesus, before time began. (1 Tim. 1:9)

Jesus has said, "My children, the plan of My Father will unfold according to the needs of the greatest number who need. God is the Father and Creator of all people, irregardless of what each one believes. There is no truth more important to you, at this time, than to realize and to believe that you are loved by your Creator beyond your imagining. Your goal should be to return to your origin, to the Father, with Me, your Jesus, under the power of Our Holy Spirit, through knowing, loving and serving the Father, His Will and His Plan."

Reflections for the Month

As Christians we need to see things in the perspective of Christ, in the perspective of the "Father Who is in Heaven," from Whom Jesus, our Lord, was sent and to Whom He has returned. The whole of Christian life is like a great "pilgrimage to the house of the Father," whose unconditional love for every human creature, and in particular for the "prodigal son," we discover anew each day. This pilgrimage takes place in the heart of each person and extends to the believing community and then to the whole of humanity.

God is Love! God is Mercy! God's mercy is unconditional love and forgiveness. When we have received God's mercy and love, and have accepted it, we in turn then must show this mercy and love to others, to ourselves and to God. We must remember that God's mercy is greater than sin! Mercy is the greatest attribute of God. The only answer to the dreadful state and condition of the world is the **Mercy of God.**

This "journey to the Father" should encourage everyone to undertake an authentic conversion, by holding fast to Christ the Redeemer of man. When we are centered on the person of Christ, this become a great act of praise to the Father: "Blessed be the God and Father of our lord Jesus Christ, Who has blessed us in Christ, with every spiritual blessing, in the heavenly places, even as He chose us in Him, before the foundation of the world, that we should be holy and blameless before Him." (Eph.1:3-4)

(Some of above taken from Pope John Paul's Apostolic Letter, *Tertio Millennio Adveniente*.)

Prayer

Heavenly Father, through the heart of Your beloved Son, Jesus, our Lord and Savior, I come before you in all humility and beg your forgiveness for offenses, my sins, which have hurt you and ask, through Jesus Your Son, for Your mercy and love, which I in turn will then show to my brothers and sister, to You and to myself. I praise and thank you for all You are doing in my life, and I ask that you take my will and make it Your Will in all things. Amen.

Resolution

During this month I want to practice the virtue of charity more, because without charity I cannot receive love and mercy and cannot give this to others, to God or to myself. I know that Charity is in all reality the love of God and neighbor and is the summing up of the moral life of the believer. Charity has in God its source and its goal. I will learn of the Father, through listening to the Holy Spirit and through what Jesus has taught me about Our Father. I will consecrate myself, totally, not only to Jesus through the heart of Mary, to the Holy Spirit, but also to my Father, the Almighty and Holy One, my Creator.

Meditations For August

Focus: God the Father

"Only in God is my soul at rest; from Him comes my salvation. He only is my rock and my salvation, my stronghold; I shall not be disturbed. With God is my safety and my glory, He is the rock of my strength; my refuge is in God. Trust in Him at all times, O my people! Pour out your hearts before Him; God is our refuge!" (Psalm 62: 2,7-9)

August 1   (Feast – St. Alphonsus Liquori, Bishop/Doctor) Mission for Souls

(**Jesus speaks**) My beloved ones, the plan of the Father for each of you is perfect and will unroll as a set of occurrences that are perfectly balanced and perfectly laid out. You will be led to an understanding of **"Father."** My dear ones, there is now, more than ever, a need for intense prayer and time spent before Me in the Blessed Sacrament. Know that all is well for you in this plan of Our Father. Be grateful to My Father, and yours, for His gifts of fidelity and perseverance.

August 2   (Feast – St. Peter Julian Eymard) Coming Closer to the Father

(**Mary speaks**) Dearest children of my heart, give thanks and praise at all times to be called children of the Most High God and of me, your loving Mother. Words from Holy Scripture, and Our words of love, joy, hope and faith are meant to lead Our children closer to Our God, the Father of all. When you desire to be one with the Father, you will see there is much unfathomable love and mercy, that only the heart, the soul, that is one with Us, can then see. The Father is all love and mercy. Please show Him, in return, your love and mercy. He will not be outdone in generosity.

August 3   Continue to Pray in Trust and Faith

(**Mary speaks**) Dear ones of My Immaculate Heart, it is so important that you continue to pray in trust and faith that the Father's Will be accomplished in you and in the entire universe. This needs to be in all of the Father's children, for He knows when it is the best time for this Will, this mercy and love of His, to be felt in each and every child of His. Be prepared to accept all with joy and thanksgiving which comes from the Father, always praising the Most Holy One, God Our Father.

August 4   (Feast — St. John Vianney)
In the Father's Love

(**Jesus speaks**) Loved ones, the Father, in His love, is doing wonderful and miraculous things in people's hearts, through Me, His Son. Do not question His methods or His reasons for anything, please. Just trust and love unconditionally. This is how you are to live from now on. He knows what each one needs to allow a full return to Him in sorrow and repentance. Do not question Him, dear ones, but wait and see. My Father's Will is always being fulfilled in each person and in the events within each of your lives. The Father's love is great for His children.

August 5   (Feast – Dedication of St. Mary of Rome) Will of the Father

(**Jesus speaks**) How you are loved, dearest ones of My Heart. Be filled with joy with this fact. Long to come into My arms forever in peace. Long to see Me, to see the Father. Allow Me to bring you into Paradise, at different times, according to My Father's Will for you. Give yourself entirely to the Will of My Father and surrender your worries and cares to Him. I am your Jesus Who praises and loves My Father with the strength contained in the Blessed and Holy Trinity. Children, love and serve all who come to you and trust that the Father's Will is being accomplished. All of your chores are little match sticks building a mighty edifice of praise and love for Our Heavenly Father!

August 6   (Feast – Transfiguration) Second Coming

(**Mary speaks**) Dearest children of mine, yes, there will be a Second Coming of My Son and soon. The soon is not to be speculated on and taken out of the context of Holy Scripture. Only God the Father of all knows when this will occur. My children, do not venture or try to decide when or how something is going to happen in the future, for this belongs to the Father and what He plans for each of you and His world. Remember, He allows many things to happen; then through prayer, events which He planned can be eliminated or lessened. You are to love and to pray in "the now, the today," and not speculate on the tomorrows.

August 7 (Ss. Cajetan & Sixtus, Pope, and Companions)
Let God do as He Knows Best

(**Mary speaks**) My precious ones, give me your prayers, uniting all with me for the tomorrows and then **let God do as He knows best.** He will never abandon you, unless you turn your backs on Him and do not soften your hardened hearts. He created all in a perfect picture of unity and love. He wishes to have this restored as He Willed it at the beginning of Creation. Know in faith and in the trust of being His little child, that He will do everything for your good, always, and for the good of all His children.

August 8 (Feast — St. Dominic)
God Knows the Hearts of Man

(**Jesus speaks**) My little children, do you believe your God sees and knows all that is in your heart? Do you know your Father, your God, wants to take care of you because of His undying, His relentless love for each of you? Do you also know that because of hardened hearts and the refusing to accept the One, true God, coming to Him in humility as His little child, that He will allow certain things to happen in His world? Do you know this will be done because He loves you and wants you only to love Him in return?

August 9 Restraints on God

(**Mary speaks**) Please, my little ones, do not put spiritual or mental restraints on your God, the Father of us all. He knows what is best for you and for all His children. Let Him be God. This is what He does best. Please, my beloved children, listen to my words to you, for they are given as a pure gift from the Father Who made us. We are His creatures and He loves us all dearly. He loves totally and invitingly, as He invites us to approach His Throne, with joy and cry out, "Abba!" The beginning of a deeper relationship with Our Creator is one of deeper simplicity, based on our littleness.

August 10   (Feast – St. Lawrence)
Relax in the Father's Care

(**Mary speaks**) My loved children, the Father's great love for us is meant to make us comfortable in His Presence, to relax in the warmth of His care and wonderful providence for our lives. Each of you, my children, more than ever, are invited to know your God as more than approachable. You should get to know Him, Who directs every action around you, for your good, bringing you most quickly to Him. Know too, children, that the Father's time is not yours, no matter what is said. Know that your docility and obedience to all that does or does not occur is central to your growth into His Divine Will. The only thing necessary for you to say at each moment is, "yes" and "Amen."

August 11   (Feast – Ss. Clare & Philomena)
Remain in Simplicity and Humility

(**Jesus speaks**) My beloved ones, the laws of My Father for His people will soon be reinstated in the hearts of all mankind. Hearts will be emptied of sin. The graces He wishes to shower upon you will blossom once again, in the Garden of His Will. My dearest ones, remain in simplicity and humility, waiting for My Father's Will to act on behalf of the world. Nothing happens until He decrees it. When you learn to let go of expectations, fears and excitement, you learn to just be in joy, peace and hope in My Father's Will, accepting all He allows to happen.

August 12   Praise Him for Everything

(**Jesus speaks**) My children, praise be to My Father Who gifts each of you with every sort of good thing. Praised be His Divine Plan for the salvation of His children. Thank and praise Him at every moment for His gracious goodness on your behalf. Give Him all the love in your hearts and think of the Most Blessed Trinity every time you think! You are then seeking unity with Me, with the Father. Praise and gratitude to the Father for His gifts, opens the way for more of His gifts! The Father's Will is being fulfilled in each person. He knows exactly what each one needs, to allow a full return to Him, in sorrow and repentance. Do not question. Wait and see, love and serve and trust that the Father's Will is being accomplished.

August 13   (Feast – Ss. Pontain & Hippolytus)
God's Relationship with You

(**Mary speaks**) My children, God is the One Who never changes. You do. His relationship with you is always the same: love, mercy and trust which are unfathomable to the human mind and heart. As your relationship grows with your God, the Father of all, you begin to see Him as the only Good you will ever need. When you get to know Him, your love and mercy toward him grows and it will grow for others and for yourself, at the same miraculous time. This is all done through prayer. He will then give much grace, through the Holy Spirit, when one asks it of Him.

August 14 (Feast – St. Maximilian Kolbe)
Know the Father Through The Son

(**God the Father speaks**) My children, if you draw near the Heart of My Son, Jesus, and know Him through His Sacred Heart, you then know My Thoughts, you know Me. Always stay in that close relationship with Jesus, My Son, dearest children, and you will know all there is to know about Me. My Heart is pure Spirit, as is My Son's. We have the Third Person of Our Trinity, Our Holy Spirit. We are One. We are One God and all works to the good of nature and in My universe, when My creation recognizes Me as God, the Creator, God of Love and Mercy.

August 15 (Feast – Assumption of Blessed Virgin Mary)
Turn Your Backs on the World

(**Jesus speaks**) I wish, as does the Father, My beloved children, to give each of you the grace to be able to decide in your free will, which is a great and loving gift from the Father (free will) to come and follow Us now today! Lay down all that is not of Us. Turn your backs on the world. Each of you must decide this for yourself: Will it be the world or Us? I am suggesting you not wait to do this, but do it TODAY! Without Our grace and a complete unity with Us, you will never be able to turn your backs on what the world has to offer.

August 16 (Feast — St. Stephen of Hungary) We Wait

(**Jesus speaks**) Beloved ones, come to Us now. We love you and wish you to be Ours Now, and for all Eternity. I bestow My peace and mercy on all who hear and read these words of Ours and then will do something about them. Ponder them! Contemplate them! Then do what your heart dictates for your decision. Decide for Us not what the world would have you understand. We are here waiting. Won't you please come into Our loving arms so We can heal you and give you all the nourishment (grace) you will ever need.

August 17 Ask The Father

(**Jesus speaks**) Beloved of My Heart, would the Father not give you all, just for the asking, when you comply to His Will? Do We not have all you will ever need? Are you filled with so much pride, arrogance and disobedience, that you feel you can handle everything yourselves? Why? My children, how you make this Sacred Heat of Mine ache! How you make the Father's Heart ache! Our Hearts ache to hold you, to love you completely and then to have you acknowledge this Love, by returning it to Us, in even a small portion.

August 18 When the Trinity Dwells in a Soul

(**God, the Father speaks**) My children, when you know the Son, the mother of the Son, you then know Me and Our Holy Spirit as well. There is no way, when One dwells in a soul, that the Others are not there as well. I am your Father.

I am God. I am Creator of all mankind, of all Creation. **I am Yahweh!** Love Me as I love you. Then once more all will be well with My world. Pray for My Son's Second Coming. Know that I do everything out of love and mercy for all of you, My creatures. You were always meant to live with Me, to see Me, to love as I love. I must and will re-create all anew. For those who have faith and love in their hearts, love and peace will reign again, very soon. Your hearts belong to Me, your Creator, the only God of all. **Follow My Son to Me!**

August 19   (Feast — St. John Eudes)
The Father's Gaze of Love

(**Jesus speaks**) Dearest children of Ours, you and I, dear children, must be inseparable, so I may work My Will, the Father's Will, in you and through you. Therefore, when the Father gazes upon Me with love, He will see and be gazing upon you with the same love. When you do Our Will, My dear ones, it is the greatest act of mercy you could perform for the world. You are being merciful to My Father in Heaven when you allow Him to work through you, His Will for His people. Without the instrument of free will to use for His purposes, the Father chooses to remain helpless. Without your willingness to obey all He asks of you, the Father could not continue His Plan of Salvation for all of creation. The Father has chosen to work through His people as instruments, of Divine Grace, Mercy and Love.

August 20   (Feast — St. Bernard, Abbot/Doctor)
Renewed Each Day

(**Jesus speaks**) Loved ones, gratitude is the key to the Heart of the Father. The morning of each day sees the world renewed, for whatever comes, according to His Will. Let each morning be a new beginning of your own preparation, for the Will of My Father. Remember dear ones, unless you say "yes" to the Father's invitation, nothing can be accomplished. It is true, you were created through no choice of your own, but you will not be saved without specific choices on your part. Everything you could ever need is completely at your disposal, but you must choose to love, to forgive, to have mercy. This is the mystery of God's Love.

August 21   (Feast — Ss. Pius X, Pope, and Jane Frances
de Chantal) Seek and You Shall Find

(**Jesus speaks**) My dearest little ones, the Wisdom of the Father is perfect! He knows each of His children completely and perfectly. The Father loves you all as though you were already in Heaven with Him. Please thank the Father for each struggle and rejection He allows you to experience, as well as for the good things in your life. Dear ones, always give the Father praise and your own love and gratitude for everything. Ask to be healed according to Our Will and it will be done. Seek and you shall find. Knock and We will open unto you. We love you!

August 22   Putting Other Needs First

(**God, the Father speaks**) My dear, dear ones, be always filled with My peace and great love for you. There is nothing greater than love which can unite Us. Even suffering, if done with joy and love and surrender, is the unity that is accomplished when two people love each other. This is possible when My grace is received by you, who put all of My needs, all My desires before your own. The more you surrender your will to Mine, the more you will have My grace and peace. I am a God of Mercy Who wishes the best for My people.

August 23   (Feast — St. Rose of Lima)
             Resistance to Grace

(**God, the Father speaks**) Loved children of Mine, since the beginning of time the lure of the senses has clouded the reality of My beauty and goodness. When the excitement of any one given moment befuddles the mind, it causes My children to lose the "Way." This is a problem of faith, dear ones. This is the result of sin and turning away from Me. The pain in the lives of My children has always been great because of the resistance offered by them to My simplicity, to My good judgment, on their behalf. Those of you who indulge each whim, each desire, will never be in My peace. This will continue until your own needs are no longer first and your own desires do not consume you. When you can dwell in thankfulness for the moment, no matter what occurs, will allow you then to overcome your struggles and gain the freedom necessary to allow My Will to work in you completely.

August 24   (Feast — St. Bartholomew, Apostle)
           Wait In Peace

(**God, the Father speaks**) Little children, anyone who wishes to serve Me must be willing to wait in peace, for Me to act in their lives. My Spirit will let you know when these times of action are to occur. I always act in your best interest. Always live in faith and trust that I am doing good for you, for all My people and for My world. My dearest ones, I long to reveal Myself more fully to all of you, if you would only allow this. Please come in simplicity and seek My Kingdom, then wait in simplicity and be grateful for every moment that has been and that will be. I promise you My love forever! Let us begin now, to walk arm in arm, in peace and simplicity, so that My joy may be yours and your joy may be complete. (note: Joy is the most infallible sign of the Presence of God.)

August 25   (Feast — St. Louis of France) God is Good

(**Jesus speaks**) Dearest children, God the Father is good, kind and merciful, because He is a loving Father. He has given you, through Me, every opportunity of seeing errors in your ways, giving you the ability to come back to Him and into His Loving Heart. Do not continue to be spiritually blind. Please start seeing with the eyes of your hearts. My children, you should always be prepared for whatever the Father has and is planning for you and for His world. **The time to do this is NOW.**

August 26   Spiritual Accidents

(**Mary speaks**) Beloved children, your knowledge of the importance of obedience will greatly help you to understand how this virtue is necessary to salvation. Without obedience to the Will of God the Father, you are like loose bearings in a machine. It runs this way and that, without proper control and often ends in a crash. Please, dear ones, avoid spiritual "accidents." Become more obedient to the Commandments, to the Beatitudes, to the Mercy that is being set before you daily, through your loving Father. To be a child of God, you must practice being childlike and dependent on the Father's care. You must trust that He will provide all that is needed in your life, all the time praising and thanking and listening to the Father.

August 27   (Feast — St. Monica) Desire to do His Will

(**Jesus speaks**) My dear, dear children, the very desire to do the Will of My Father is His gift to you. Please remember to offer each task to the Father and then thank Him, at the completion of each one. If you live in this way, you will be living in the presence of God and His Heavenly Court. This is the nearest to Paradise you can be on this earth. There is great rejoicing over all of you, My dear ones, who pray and strive to do His Will. You fill Our Hearts with joy, as We watch you struggle for patience and holiness. Please continue to struggle against your sinful nature. All will be accomplished according to the Will of My Father.

August 28   (Feast – St. Augustine)
            Perfect Union with God

(**God, the Father, speaks**) My children, I, your Heavenly Father, am calling you to greater holiness, to more prayer, to greater love for Me, for My Son, for Our Spirit, for the Beloved Mother of the Son and for all Our children in the world. Each time you say, "Thy Will be done," you are lifted higher and more blessed by My Will. Please continue to be in the most perfect union with Me, through the Sacred Heart of My Son and the Immaculate Heart of Mary. Dwell in Our peace, continually denying your self and deferring to Me. Fidelity gladdens My Heart and assures Me of your love. **Only by living out your promises can you adhere to the action of My Promises.**

August 29   (Feast – Beheading of John Baptist) Appreciation of God's Gifts

(**Mary speaks**) Beloved and cherished children, please remember appreciation of God's gifts will help you to realize more what a privilege it is to be allowed to serve God and His people. Gratitude is a necessary ingredient on your way to holiness. Appreciation makes you aware of the different gifts the Father has given you and how He is allowing you to use them. All the things we do, dear children, are a result of God's gift to us. He allows us to serve Him and each other, by using these same gifts.

August 30   The Path to Perfection

(**Jesus speaks**) Beloved children, the path you now take will be the perfect way to My Father's Will and the perfection He wishes to give you. This perfection is a docile and joyful living each moment in Our Presence. Each step you take must be in complete harmony with Our Desires. Do you not realize that what the Father has to offer, in all reality, is the only means by which you can gain the happiness and peace you are looking for? Why then, do you continue to look in the wrong places and in the wrong directions? We are here. Seek Us out and you will find Us. Please do not refuse to accept Us into your lives, into your hearts.

August 31   Praise of The Father

(**Mary speaks**) Little ones of My Heart, please remember all you have been given by God, without His Presence at every moment in your lives, you would have nothing and would be nothing. Therefore my beloved children it is fitting to give Him praise and thanksgiving for everything.

> "Praised be the Father Who gifts His children. Praise to Him Who continues to call His people to return to Him for more gifts. Praise to Him Who longs to gift us with Himself for all Eternity. Praise to Him Who allows me to come to all of you and speak to you and pray with you. Praise Him children, with every breath. Seek Him in all you do. Remain hidden with me and you will learn quickly that TO LOVE IS ALL!"

SEPTEMBER

Trust - Faith - The Will of God

"But how shall they call on Him in Whom they have believed? And how can they believe unless they have heard of Him? And how can they hear unless there is someone to preach? ... But not all have believed the gospel. Isaiah asks, 'Lord, who has believed what he has heard from us?' Faith then, comes through hearing, and what is heard is the word of Christ." (Romans 10:14,16-17)

We are created to live a life of Christ, in all its dimensions. We are meant to receive the eternal rewards earned for us, by His Passion and Death and Resurrection. All the graces we require are here, for the asking, are ours for the taking, and will be given in overabundance, if we but ask. All that is needed is to turn to Jesus and Mary, in complete trust and faith, turning our very "selves" over to Them in total surrender to the Will of God. Great joy will then be felt by living this way, as we will be further convinced to persevere in our journey towards grace and power and the gifts from the Father in Heaven, Who meant to save us from all of eternity. We will be further convinced that we need to follow Him, our Jesus, on that road that leads to holiness, our sainthood, our eternal life with Them in Heaven. Let us then, respond to the Most Holy Trinity, to Mary, our Mother, with all our minds, all our hearts, all our souls and all our strength and wills.

Reflection for the Month

Jesus is asking: "My beloved ones, I love and **AM LOVE. Please love LOVE in return!** Please **trust** in Our care for you. Continue to pray, to persevere and to remain close to Me. Continue to work and live the way you have been, doing all in a schedule that includes balance and peace. Remember children, I am your God, the One Who has saved you already. Please, just allow yourselves to continue to trust, in faith, all We have told you, that you know to be truth.

"My children, please remember, Holy Scripture is truth and can be trusted. When you read Scripture, I would recommend you call on the Holy Spirit to enlighten your minds and hearts, to know what the meaning of a particular part, or all, of scripture is for you, in this present age. Then pray to know and understand what scripture is calling you to do and what you are being called to. My Words are written through the prophets, disciples and apostles, and were all divinely inspired by your God, through the working of Our Holy Spirit, Who dwells in all souls and hearts, in the degree with which He is welcomed or is not welcomed. He it is that inspires your souls to heights that can only be grasped when a soul is open to Him."

The Blessed Mother has repeatedly, in all her pleadings, said: *"My children, please abandon all to Jesus. You must have complete **trust, love and faith.** Come to the Foot of the Cross where many mysteries will unfold. Follow Jesus. Your hearts, your souls, your wills are what He wants. This is the key: When you give all to Us, you will see wonderful and miraculous happenings."*

Prayer

My God, I believe, I adore, I hope, I trust and I love you. Thy will be done in me for I wish no longer to have my will exist, only Your Will within me, for I will nothing except that which you desire of me. I believe in faith, but help my unbelief, that all that you have planned for me is the best that could ever be. Thank you for loving me so much. Amen.

Resolution

No matter how many times I will fall this month in my trust and faith towards what the Father is planning for my life, I will to get up again, and again, to try once more to live the Will of God in all that I think, say and do.

Meditations For September

Trust — Faith — Will of God

"There is, to be sure, a certain wisdom which we express among the spiritually mature. It is not a wisdom of this age, however, nor of the rulers of this age, who are men headed for destruction. No, what we utter is God's wisdom: a mysterious, a hidden wisdom. God planned it before all ages for our glory. None of the rulers of this age knew the mystery; if they had known it, they would never have crucified the Lord of glory. Of this wisdom it is written: 'Eye has not seen, ear has not heard, nor has it so much as dawned on man what God has prepared for those who love Him.'"
(1 Corinthians 2:6-9)

September 1 Believe in Faith

(Jesus speaks) My loved little children, when you believe (in trust) all We wish and will of you and as you learn to live this trust, in complete surrender and love of the Father, you begin to grow in the fullness of faith. When you trust in complete surrender to Me, a complete giving to Me, of your very selves, your faith will grow and become as a shining light to all who need to see Me, through you. It is My desire that you learn complete trust and have total confidence in Me.

September 2   The Only Way

(**Jesus speaks**) Children of My Merciful Heart, say often, **"Jesus, I trust in You,"** until your whole being believes and accepts this fact. There is no longer time for deciding whether you can or want to do this. **You must, My little ones, as I am the only Way, the only Light you will be able to follow out of this sea of darkness.** It is imperative you not waver in this faith you have in Me; that your trust is complete. You will need to be a beacon of light to others.

September 3   (Feast – St. Gregory the Great) Joy in Faith

(**Mary speaks**) My loved ones, the need is more than ever for a complete trust, as you wait in patient faith for many things in your lives. You need a faith built on the solid ground of: wisdom, perseverance, trust and patience. When things in your life seem impossible, it is then you are to trust even more. It is then you are to acknowledge all that comes from God is good and only good can come from His Plans for you. Encourage within yourself and in others, strength and the conviction of faith in the one, true God. You must learn of His love and mercy, let joy fill your very beings so that one looking at you will see Jesus' Light, His Love, and all will be well.

September 4   Importance of Faith and Trust

(**Mary speaks**) My beloved children, you are now to go about your daily tasks in my spirit, that is, the spirit of humility, obedience, trust, faith, joy and hope. We need your constant "Fiats" in complete **trust and faith.** Know that you are needed by Us and will be called on to do many things. Each of you are in the Palm of His Hand, when you have given me yourselves and once you have died to the self that wants control, that doesn't want to let go of pride. No matter where you are in the plan of the Father, you must be ready to accept all in **trust and faith** that what is being asked of you is according to His Will and in your best interest. Each of you is a piece in this salvation puzzle of the Father's. In order to fit perfectly, you need to be in complete submission and readiness at all times.

September 5   Priorities

(**Jesus speaks**) My beloved ones, please, put your priorities in the right perspectives. Ask Me. Talk with Me. It is only then that you will receive the answers you need and are looking for. Keep in My Peace and My Joy. Trust is the word I have taught for so long. TRY IT, it does work. I bless each of you now who read this and take it to heart and then take it to prayer, as then My Heart will speak to your heart. Keep your focus, your priorities in line with Me, with My Will, and all will then go according to My Will for you. **I am with you always. Let hope and joy permeate your beings and you will know My Presence.**

September 6   Do Not Fear

(**Jesus speaks**) Little ones of My Sacred Heart, I am your God. I long to hold you in My loving Heart. I am here to bless, to heal, to love, to dispel the doubts that arise. I know your needs and when your need becomes a "true need" and not just a want. Let Me act in you as I know is best for you. DO NOT FEAR. There is nothing to be afraid of if we are one, you and Me, through the Immaculate Heart of your Mother Mary. **Be prepared always, to the point of complete TRUST and then let FAITH rule every fiber in your being.**

September 7   Letting Go

(**Jesus speaks**) My dearest children, when you pray the prayer, "I firmly trust and commit myself entirely to Your Holy Will, which is mercy Itself," this pleases Me very much. Do you realize what you are saying and what you have given Me? Do you realize the magnitude of these words? When you give Me all to do with as I Will, you then "let go" of everything, not only in that moment, but for that day and the days ahead. Each time you make that decision of free will, giving Me free rein to use you, as I see is best, pleases Me. This is not only for you, but for the souls I wish to use your consent for, to help them, even unknowingly, for a complete change of heart, in their conversion.

September 8   (Feast — Birth of Virgin Mary)
Hold Fast and Firm in Faith

(**Bl. Faustina speaks**) My dearest sisters and brothers, I resisted for quite awhile coming to Him and giving myself wholly and completely to Him, in a firm, lasting trust. When you finally decide to give all to Him, wonders then are created within your interior self, in your soul; Transformations take place, not only in your interior castle, but to your entire exterior house as well. Always do this, as it will insure the peace, the grace you will need for the times that lie ahead. **Hold fast and firm in your faith, always trusting everything to Him, to Mary our Immaculate Mother.**

September 9   (Feast — St. Peter Claver)
              Impulse of True Love

(**Jesus speaks**) Dear ones, I no longer want you to act except by the impulse of My pure love. If I am truly to take everything you have and are, then to transform you into Myself, I must be able to use you as My Heart wishes and desires, from this moment on. Please surrender "you" today. Surrender the complete you, entirely to My pleasure and Will. You will do this until one day you no longer need to, as you will then be adoring Me and basking in My brilliant Light and Love for all Eternity. Continue to trust in faith. See Me in all you do.

September 10 Wisdom and Faith

(**Jesus speaks**) My beloved children, please try to see from your heart and understand that all wisdom comes from the Father. Wisdom is not something that can be acquired like a new pair of shoes. No, wisdom comes from Our Hearts (the Triune God) to your hearts. Then to possess faith is the discovering of a great treasure. It takes prayer for the grace to be able to have this wisdom which enhances and builds on your Faith. Faith is not something that can be given through the world. **Faith and Wisdom** in the world are but folly. Faith, and the wisdom to know how to acquire this faith, is God given.

September 11   Gift From the Father

(**Jesus speaks**) My children, wisdom and faith are gifts. They are the greatest gifts of mercy and love which the Father bestows on hearts, on souls who wish to accept this treasure. It is free, but only in the sense that you then go into the world, which is in such darkness, and show by your lives, by your actions, what it is and what it means to live as one with Us in love, mercy, faith, joy and hope. Live joy and hope in complete trust and perseverance. Live simply, out of a complete turning to Me through Wisdom. Through this you will find a strengthening and enlightenment of your faith.

September 12   Not to Hesitate

(**Mary speaks**) Dear, dear little ones, faith must be built by following whatever the Will of God appears to be, at the moment, without hesitation and without conditions. Bring your emotions to Jesus and to me. We can heal you and calm your inner turmoil. Trials are just that. Trials leave you feeling inadequate, puzzled and helpless. This is designed to place your focus on God and His power and shows your own lack of it. When you are completely dependent on God for all things, you will experience this and will never be able to miss the fact that He is God and will provide for everything.

September 13   (Feast – St. John Chrysostom)
Dependence on Jesus

(**Jesus speaks**) My precious ones, wisdom comes from much prayer to Me and with Me, through a communion of

Our Hearts and your utter dependence on Me for everything. These are important steps in Wisdom of Faith. You need patience. You need Trust; You need Me, all through Mary and Joseph. Depend on Me. Die to yourself so My Spirit can work in you, to accomplish this stronghold of faith. Faith is likened to a castle or fortress built on high ground, which is impenetrable. It is firm. It is solid. It is strong: The same it is with faith. This stronghold of faith in each of your hearts and souls cannot be build without the wisdom to know how, when and why it is being built. You need a master architect and builder. I AM that Architect and Builder. The price is high: your souls given to Me in the same trust, love and joy I give to you.

September 14 (Feast — The Holy Cross) Gift of Free Will

(Jesus speaks) My dearest and most loved ones, the darkness of the soul are anxieties, depression, anger, self-love, ego, resentments, self-pity, impatience, impurities of any kind. These are food for the "self" (self-love) and turn into a "feeling sorry" for oneself (self-pity). This must be dealt with firmly and with trust in My love and mercy for you. Give it all to Me. I will take care of all your needs. Children, exercise the great gift of free will and unite your will with My Will, giving all to Me. All My teachings from the beginning of time are based on the great commandment of love. I plead with you, My children, to please "trust Me to be God" and to do what is best for you. Start thinking with your hearts, with My Heart, with Mother Mary's Heart. Give Us your will freely and let Us help you in everything. Do not put obstacles in the way of your soul achieving holiness.

September 15   (Feast – Our Lady of Sorrows)
                   One That Listens

(**Jesus speaks**) My children, **wisdom of faith** is something to be grasped at and prayed for. It is something most important to find, to want. It is a lesson learned which is simplistic. It will prove to your soul the worthiness of endurance of faith through the wisdom given to each soul, when it is asked for. To accept it, you need to be an open vessel, one that listens, instead of doing, doing and being busy constantly, as when the Holy Spirit comes, He comes to the silence of a heart, a soul, and He rests there, if He is welcomed. He cannot stand the hustle-bustle of the world.

September 16   (Feast – St. Cornelius, Pope
                   & St. Cyprian, Bishop) The Keys

(**Jesus speaks**) Loved ones, the keys to a firm structure of faith through wisdom are: purity of heart, state of grace, repentance and reconciliation with Me, with each other and with yourself, the sacraments, which I instituted for your sanctification. Then there is My Holy Word and the Truth which My holy shepherd, your Pope John Paul teaches. He is able to teach you because of his firm and deeply rooted wisdom of faith. Without **Wisdom of Faith** you will never find the truth as you will always be blinded by what the world would have you believe is truth.

September 17 (Feast – St. Robert Bellarmine)
The Wisdom of Faith

(**Jesus speaks**) My beloved children, you cannot do as I Will for you unless you wait in patience and trust for Me to enlighten you; unless you know I am always with you. I know when it is the right time for you to receive the graces of Wisdom of Faith. I do My part always. I never change! Now you need to do your part to become one with Me and like Me. You will know when you have the **Wisdom of Faith** by your love, your joy, your trust and your humility. Wisdom of Faith is likened to a child who rarely questions, accepts in trust, in love, in faith and does all in joy and gladness of heart. Will you seek this great grace of having The Wisdom of Faith?

September 18 (Feast – St. Joseph of Cupertino)
Pearl of Rare Beauty

(**St. Joseph speaks**) Children of the Holy Family, as I learned to turn myself entirely over to my God in everything, my spiritual strength grew within me, so much so, that when I was to take Mary as my wife, I was confused as I found she was already with child. But I turned to God in much suppliant prayer and He sent His Angel to calm my fears and my heart. I was learning to become strong in the wisdom of my faith. I was being taught wisdom through a source I knew not, but I trusted and my faith did not waver. The grace of wisdom is a priceless treasure, **a pearl of rare beauty.** Wisdom should be nurtured. It will grow and will feed faith, giving you a strong sense of oneness with us, the Holy Family.

September 19 (Feast — Our Lady of LaSalette & St. Janarius, Bishop) Path of Truth

(**Jesus speaks**) My beloved children, with faith, do everything being asked of you, only one day at a time, each day. Stand firm in your faith, your hope and your trust. Be strong of heart, of mind and of will, spirit and feelings. I am always here for you. I love you with a love that will never cease and is not comprehensible. I beg you to trust in faith all I ask of you. This cannot be done without the grace from Me. Ask it of Me and it shall be given you and then you must live it. You are to trust My Words in Holy Scripture. Through keeping your focus on Me, on My teachings through My Church, through what your Pope John Paul teaches will keep you on the path of truth.

September 20 Perfect Plan

(**St. Joseph speaks**) My children, when you understand that what God has planned for you and your loved ones is perfect, even things that to your mortal heart may not seem so at the time, all will be well. Give all to Him saying, "so be it," Your Will, not mine, is what I desire now and for all time. Then let Him do as He knows is best for you and yours, for His world. As I learned long ago, trust Him with a faith that cannot be shaken and all will be well. Keep in faith, in the wisdom of faith, that your God knows what is best for you in all situations. Keep close to us, the Holy Family now and always. Keep these words of love and encouragement in your heart from your Father St. Joseph who loves you very much.

September 21 (Feast — St. Matthew, Apostle)
Gateway to Joy

(**Jesus speaks**) Dear ones of My Sacred Heart, the Father's plan for you requires only your "yes" and ongoing cooperation. Please have a deep conviction and a total confidence in My love and care for you. This will be your peace. Live in My peace and in My love for you. This then will help fulfill the Father's Will for you. Surrendering to the Will of the Father is the Gateway to Joy! It is the narrow path which leads to the heart of the Kingdom. With it comes peace and contentment and security like you have never imagined. These are gifts deep within the soul and are the result of allowing My Heavenly Father to lead you in determining your life events according to what He knows is best for you and your soul. This enables the soul to come most quickly to a state of perfection and unity with the Holy Trinity.

September 22 Leading to the Divine Will

(**Mary speaks**) Dear ones, on your journey to the Father, it will lead you to His Divine Will. Divine Will is LOVE. It is absolute. It is mercy beyond human comprehension. It is possible to be submissive to His Will and in harmony with Him, the Creator, at all times. You need to travel this journey to the Divine Will by travelling away from what the world would have you believe as being the ultimate joy, happiness and love. Through my Immaculate Heart you will learn to be submissive to His Will and how it is possible to find the Kingdom on earth and a closeness to the Creator as was always planned by Him.

September 23 Important Element

(**Mary speaks**) Children of My Heart, being in the state of sanctifying grace is a most important element to accomplish His Will for you in your life. He cannot deal with a soul who rejects Him by sin and that is exactly what happens when you are not in the state of grace. When you are able to see with the eyes of the heart and the eyes of the soul, you will see Heaven and know that the reward awaiting you far outweighs anything else in this journey to Eternal Life with Us.

September 24 Living in Trust

(**Jesus speaks**) My beloved children, when you live in Our Will in Trust, you will be able to endure much suffering as I did for souls, for the salvation of many and for yourself. You will never question what is being asked of you but will do all in love, peace and in the simple faith of a child whose eyes are focused on the One it adores, admires, loves and Whom it trusts completely. You will trust in blind obedience all I give you. You will do all I ask, because your will, will no longer exist. Only Our Will will exist within you, because you have willed it so.

September 25 Giving of Oneself

(**Jesus speaks**) Dear ones, when Our Will exists within you completely, the Triune God will live completely and in total harmony with you; with your thoughts, your feelings, with your heart and with your soul. To give of oneself is not of the human nature because of Original Sin. As you learn to know Me, to lean on Me, to love Me above all else, including your very self, you will begin to believe in faith, with the wisdom of that simple, humble childlike trust in Me and Me alone.

September 26 (Feast — St. Cyprian & Ss. Isaac Joques and Companions) Greatest Gift

(**Jesus speaks**) Dearest ones of My Heart, pray with Mary, your mother, and St. Joseph often, asking them to take charge of your very person, your hearts, your wills and to show you how to submit, to abandon completely, to My Will. The adversary hates a soul who is fashioned in Divine Will and he will hate you who are doing and living My Divine Mercy. Do not falter. It is a rugged path but the reward is the greatest gift you will ever receive. Come then, when you feel you are ready, to enclose yourself in the Divine Will of the Most Holy Trinity.

September 27 (Feast — Ss. Vincent De Paul, Cosmos & Damien) Supple Flowers

(**Jesus speaks**) Dear ones, be like supple flowers blowing in the breeze of Our Spirit. Allow yourself to be sent in whatever direction is willed by My Father and you will soon feel more comfortable living in this freedom. The Light of the World will then shine from within your heats. Allow yourself to be more and more emptied and then dear ones, to be filled with My Presence, that My Light may indeed shine upon all, through you.

September 28 (Feast – St. Wenceslaus) Greater Union

(**Mary speaks**) My dearest children, spend your days in prayer and in greater union with Our Two Hearts and the Father's Will for you. Much wisdom will be poured out on you, by the Holy Spirit, if you accept this grace. My Son, Jesus, talks often of unity and love. This must be, before there is peace of any kind. Listen to Him. He is The Truth and The Way that will take you to the Eternal Light. There must be, my little children, unity among you, my children and within my Church. There is no longer time for egos, for pride; only time for love to unify all my children. Peace will reign, as will hope, love and joy if you trust. Trust in true humility of heart. Be love! Show love!

September 29 (Feast – Ss. Michael, Gabriel & Raphael) Abandon Yourself to Him

(**St. Margaret Mary speaks**) My brothers and sisters, when you decide to abandon yourself completely to Him, to His heart, how precious your hearts and souls become to Jesus. When you take your littleness, your nothingness, your weaknesses, your sorrows and give them all to Him, for His good pleasure, He will not only heal you, but will heal this world so in need of Him and His Healing Heart.

September 30 (Feast – St. Jerome, Priest/Doctor) Be Content in Their Will

(**Jesus speaks**) My beloved children, please do not seek anything other than My Will for you. Whatever We request of you is the result of the Father's Will for your life. If you would live that Will totally, you would not ask questions regarding the future, but would wait in humble obedience. Docility is a difficult virtue. Only with the help of the Virgin Mother will you be able to live in this manner. Children, forsake all others. This does not mean you do not love them or will not serve them. You love and serve Me, when you do it for them. This means, that no other desires should fill your hearts, than to be united to Me and My desires for you. We must be inseparable now, that I may work My Will, the Father's Will in you and through you. Then, when the Father gazes upon Me with love, He will see and be gazing upon you, with the same love.

OCTOBER

Holiness and Virtues

"Blessed be the Lord, the God of Israel, because He has visited and ransomed His people... He has raised a horn of saving strength for us in the house of David His servant, as He promised through the mouths of His holy ones, the prophets of ancient times: Salvation from our enemies and from the hands of all our foes ... He has dealt mercifully with our fathers and remembered the holy covenant He made, the oath He swore to Abraham, our father, He would grant us: that, rid of fear and delivered from the enemy, we should serve Him devoutly and through all our days, be holy in His sight..." (Luke 1:68-75)

It is recommended you meditate and reflect on what Zechariah is praying in this canticle of his to God the Father. We were created to be Saints; to be Holy, as Jesus and Mary have said many a time, is something all should be striving for every day of our lives.

The Blessed Mother has said, "run to me, to My Immaculate Heart and there you will find shelter. Seek me, seek Jesus and you will find what is necessary for all your needs, your doubts, your misgivings and for your growth in Holiness. The dawn of each new day will bring a need for greater awareness of the need to consecrate each word of yours, each conversation, to the Honor and Glory of God. This will increase your awareness and sharpen your protection against proud words of conceit or boastfulness. The tone of voice with which you speak to each other can, indeed, be a healing or one that is most hurtful. You should have no wish to harm anyone, my children."

Think about being Consecrated to Jesus, to the Father, to the Holy Spirit, all through the Immaculate Heart of the One all Three have chosen – Mary, the Virgin Mother. When you are consecrated to "Them" you become Christ-like, Christ centered, Christ for the world and you become Eucharist. Reflect on this. Someone who is holy once said, "A life not fully reflected upon, is a life not fully lived." Therefore, if you do not take the time to reflect on holiness, on virtue, on God, on anything of a spiritual walk, it would seem that you then do not fully understand or full appreciate that which needs reflection.

Reflection for the Month

This same holy person said, "When we reflect on Jesus' Life, we realize all that He did and said, is a pattern for our own personal lives, (or should be) but it is also for the Church as a Body. We believe that the Church is the Mystical Body of Christ. It is actually Christ's Body alive today, living in us, helping each of us achieve the degree of holiness which was meant to be for us individually." It is good to remember that the door that opens directly to Jesus' Sacred Heart, to His Mercy, Love and Grace (as well as the door for the Holy Spirit) is through the Immaculate Heart of Mary. It has always been that way and shall continue to be, until the end of time. Our constant and consistent Consecration to the Sacred Heart of Jesus through Mary's Immaculate Heart, will be the key to finding Him, to pleasing Him, to being fully united with Jesus. This means HOLINESS; this is the means to Heaven. The perfect refuge of safety is Jesus' Heart through the Heart of the Immaculate One.

Prayer

Dearest mother of mine, Mother of God, today I entrust to you, to your Immaculate Heart, all that I am, all that I have, all that I will ever have, as I want to do everything in you, with you, through you and for you, because then I know I will be doing everything this day, in Jesus, with Jesus, through Jesus and for Jesus, all for the Honor and Glory of God. Pray with me to your Spouse, the Holy Spirit that He will give me all the necessary graces this day on my walk to becoming a saint, for my holiness. Amen.

Resolution

On my own, dear mother mine, I know I am nothing… but, with your help, I can pattern myself after your life and what you are teaching me about your Son, Jesus, and how to become more Christ-like in my behavior, in my daily life. I want to become a Saint, dear mother, and this means to become holy. Holiness is what I will strive for in special ways this month.

Special Meditations on the Virtues

These words from Jesus and Mary on the Virtues we felt important to have before you started the days of the month of October, focusing on the virtues and holiness. These words of Theirs are put here because of their importance for daily living. From the graces which the Holy Spirit imparts to our souls, through His holy gifts and the virtues which come from these gifts, will be given to each as a guideline on the road to holiness.

Jesus and Mary have this to say about various virtues needed in our lives. *"When you are broken and remolded, some parts of your 'self' are left out and replaced by virtues and new strength."*

*"Children, We know how hard it is to live in complete **Humility and Obedience,** but as you continue to try, the grace will come to accomplish all according to the plan of the Father and His Will."*

*(**Jesus**) "The **Obedience** you practice, dear children, is a catalyst for more graces to be received and My power to be experienced in each of your lives. Be grateful to the Father for His gifts of **Fidelity and Perseverance.**"*

*(**Mary**) "Beloved children, you are now to go about your daily tasks in my spirit, that is, in the spirit of **Humility, Obedience, Trust, Faith, Joy and Hope,** knowing that you are needed by all of Us and will be called on soon to do great things."*

(Mary) *"Dearest of my Heart, **Humility** is a precious virtue. It is a love virtue filled with mercy for your God, for me, for each other and for yourselves. When you have **Humility** you are blest, you are holy as He is Holy. Where true **Humility** of heart exists, He is always there, for there is no longer any sign of pride. You have then died to yourself. You no longer have your ego to contend with, that 'self-image.' **Humility** is the virtue I wish you would strive for the most. **Humility** is to be meek and humble of heart in all things. Look to my Son's Heart, to my heart and seek refuge there, in Our Hearts. Learn from me, your mother, who wants to teach you everything there is to know of how to please God."*

(Mary) *"When you are **Righteous,** dear ones, for God, your resentments and judgments fall away completely, as then you see others as I do, as the Trinity sees them, as children of God. No matter how difficult this may be, you must be able to control and put aside your feelings about people that are negative and ask yourself, how do Mary and Jesus see them? How do they love them? Then act towards them in that manner."*

(Mary) *"Children, you practice the virtue of **Prudence** by trusting and by listening to the Holy Spirit, not by acting rashly or impatiently. With **Prudence,** caution is recommended. Both prudence and caution should be exercised. This then is called a **Holy Caution and Prudence.** Many good judgments come from **Prudence.** Sometimes **Prudence** is overshadowed by enthusiasm. It is not wrong to have enthusiasm, but one must, with the use of **Prudence,** as with enthusiasm, sit back and wait for **Prudence** to dictate to your emotions. When one seeks **Prudence,** it must be done diligently and not in haste or in worry or fear."*

Meditations for October

Holiness and Virtue

"That divine power of His has freely bestowed on us everything necessary for a life of genuine piety, through knowledge of Him Who called us by His own glory and power... This is reason enough for you to make every effort to undergird your virtue with faith, your discernment with virtue, and your self-control with discernment; this self-control, in turn, should lead to perseverance, and perseverance to piety, and piety to care for your brother, and care for your brother, in love."
(2 Peter 1:3, 5-8)

October 1 (Feast — St. Therese of Child Jesus)
Unparalleled Treasure

(**Holy Spirit speaks**) Dear children, My gifts and virtues (fruits) that come from these gifts, are a treasure of unparalleled worth and value. There should be nothing upper-most in your mind other than to strive for these gifts, which I will give when you will need them. I know when it is time and when a soul is ready to receive a grace, a gift and it is then here for the asking. Unless you ask, it goes unused within you. You are to continue, unceasingly, to pray for grace, Sanctifying Grace.

October 2   (Feast of Guardian Angels)
                 Grace of Charity and Wisdom

(**Holy Spirit speaks**) Children, you need to pray continually for the virtue of Charity. Through prayer and your will to conquer all that goes against charity, you will be able to overcome being judgmental, critical, gossiping against others, blaming others and rectifying yourself in your eyes. You will conquer envy and resentments with the grace of Charity; you will become meek and humble of heart as the Hearts of Jesus and Mary. Follow Their examples, as well as those of the great Saints who have gone before you. With the grace you receive for the virtue of Charity, you will learn Prudence. Your righteousness will now turn to be a holy righteousness in Our army of souls. It is good to constantly pray for an increase of Faith, especially the Wisdom of Faith; this wisdom and understanding will come, and so will much perseverance on your part prevail.

October 3   Overcoming Sinfulness

(**Holy Spirit speaks**) My children, you must continually pray for Humility and Obedience, in order to conquer the evil head of self that would like to control you. Always try hard to obtain the grace of Patience and Discernment. Continue on this quest as much peace is given a soul who has patience and discernment. Come to Me, the Holy Spirit of the Father and the Son, when temptation arises. I dwell in hearts and souls who wish My Light and the grace of My gifts, which I want to give in much abundance. When your will is given to Us, My Will then dwells within you. Please never put obstacles in the way of this as you then bar Us from your soul, your heart and your mind.

October 4   (Feast — St. Francis of Assisi)
Holiness in the Family

(**St. Joseph speaks**) My wonderful families, I would urge you, all families, to come to a heart decision to pray more openly with each other, with us, as the Holy Family and with our God, the Father, the Son and the Holy Spirit. You will find as you do more of this, you begin to open your hearts as He wishes from all His children to do. Oh the wonderful progress you will then make in holiness, as you mature in your prayer lives. I am not telling you there will never be a crisis or problems facing you, either personally or in your family, but it becomes easier to accept because you know you have God where you want Him and exactly where He wants to be: in your hearts, in your lives and in your homes.

October 5   Practice of Virtues

(**Mary speaks**) Dear children, please seek me; seek Jesus more often. Slow down in your ways of doing things. We have all you need. Lean on Us. Trust Us. Have faith and confidence in Us. Love, trust, faith and prayer will overcome all obstacles. When you practice the virtues you need, you will see self vanish, gradually, and the 'self' that needs to die will be replaced by the virtues that are needed. The prince of darkness loves those who center on self and forget the virtues. With the practice of virtue, you will find the path to holiness much easier.

October 6   (Feast – St. Bruno & Bl. Marie-Rose Durocher) Root Out All Sin

(**Jesus speaks**) Dear children of My Sacred and Merciful Heart, there is not one facet of you that We (the Holy Trinity) do not want to abide in, but cannot unless you have rooted out sin, all desire of the flesh, all faults and have replaced them with the virtues. You have to die completely to your old selves, the self that loves things in and of the world. To be in the world, and not of it, is something all should strive for.

October 7   (Feast – Our Lady of The Rosary) Grace to Die to Self

(**Jesus speaks**) Dear ones, when you ask for the grace to die to self, obtained through prayer, sacrifice and disciplining yourselves, you will experience a gradual fading away in your lives of wanting and doing this or that. The material things will no longer have a hold over you. You will want to pray more, spend more time with Me in the Blessed Sacrament, receive Me more frequently in the Holy Eucharist. You will nourish yourselves completely with Me, living wholly for Me and in Me. **This must done every day.**

October 8   Decision to Unite Yourself with Jesus

(**Jesus speaks**) My precious children, there has to be a decision made by you to die to the flesh and live according to the Spirit. A decision to unite yourself, your will with My Will, every day and then pray, pray, pray that the Holy Spirit will shower you with the graces of His gifts. Through the grace you receive, you will be able to continue daily to die to self. You will find added strength and courage that will enable you to grow in holiness. You will find you have additional armor to withstand the evil one's strongest wiles and temptations.

October 9 (Feast – St. Denis and Companions & St. John Leonardi) Way of Holiness

(**Jesus speaks**) My dear children, you who strive for holiness, for perfection must learn to follow Me, learn of Me and learn from Me. Keep your focus always on Me, on My Cross. Suffer with Me and give all to My Virgin Mother for your protection, under Her Mantel and be within Her Immaculate Heart at all times. She then gives all of you to Me as a polished and bright treasure, for My Heart to love in Its unfathomable way. It is the way of My Heart's mercy. So trust, give all of your selves, totally, your bodies, hearts, minds, souls and wills, all through Mary Immaculate, where all joy peace, love and happiness will abound always.

October 10 See With the Heart

(**Jesus speaks**) Dear ones of My Heart, I gave you eyes to see, but also a heart to see with. If something goes directly to your heart and a change takes place, you become peaceful. You then will be walking with Me and listening with the ears of your heart and seeing with the eyes of your heart. You will use the things of this world as if you were not using them at all. You will have rejected the world and Satan. Your focus is off you and back on Me, where it belongs. You will have chosen to live with Me, in Me and through Me, You then have died to yourself.

October 11 As Little Children

(**Jesus speaks**) My beloved children, you need to become little in My Eyes, so I can give you the love that I want to share with you. To become little is to die to self each day, every minute of the day. You then can truly respond to this love of Mine, as a little child, in trust and in complete abandonment to Me, to what I Will for you. When you are small in the eyes of the world and have become like little children, I can then mold you and shape you into models of Myself and of My Mother's Heart. I can do many wonders in you, in your hearts and souls.

October 12 Miracles

(**Jesus speaks**) My loved ones, as grace flows steadily from My Heart to yours (when you allow this), miracles are wrought, souls are saved and then nothing is impossible. You **MUST** become small, nothing in your eyes, in the eyes of the world, so I can become your strength, giving you graces, through My Mother, as the Mediatrix of all Grace. This you will need in order to live in holiness, to become like Me and to prepare yourself for Sainthood and for your Eternal Home in Heaven. You are Mine, all who are small and little in the eyes of the world and in worldly thoughts. You have become giants in My Heart and in the Heart of the Father Who loves you so much.

October 13   Your Perfection

(**St. Margaret Mary speaks**) My sisters and brothers, Jesus had given me many thoughts on how one is to die to oneself in order to become as the child He always wanted, the child that was created in His Image and Likeness. You must conform yourself as closely as possible to His humility and His gentleness in dealing with your neighbor. Love those who humble and contradict you, for they are more useful to your perfection than those who flatter you. Jesus went further with me, in this teaching to my heart, that we must endeavor to the utmost of our power to enter into the adorable Heart of Our Lord by making ourselves very little and humbly confessing our nothingness, thus we lose sight of self entirely.

October 14   (Feast — St. Callistus I, Pope)
Humbled for His Name

(**Jesus speaks**) My precious children, when you remain focused on Me, on My Cross, you will see how being humbled and contradicted for My name will bring you closer to holiness and to perfection. You who strive for holiness in a complete dying to self. You must be courageous and strong in not giving way to depression, because of faults or the humiliations you encounter each day. I know it goes against your human natures to be humbled, but dear ones, it is a means for your perfection. Being humbled is a means of mercy. For some this will be most difficult. But, pray dear children, and call on the Holy Spirit for the grace you will need to persevere in this and all else you will need to acquire holiness.

October 15 (Feast — St. Teresa of Avila) Holy Spirit's Guidance

(Holy Spirit speaks) My children, I am the Spirit of God the Father and God the Son. Once a heart, a soul, has given itself to Me, to help, to guide, to direct, as We Will for it, there is nothing that the soul then cannot attain, in the Kingdom here and in Heaven. You then will be united with Us, for all Eternity, as one with Us, with all the Angels and all the Saints who have gone before you. Come then and drink from the water of salvation, in reconciliation, for the salvation of your soul and the souls We give to you, to help Us with.

October 16 (Feast — Ss. Margaret Mary Alacoque & Hedwig) To Truly Know Yourself

(Holy Spirit speaks) My children, there is a grace that We wish to give all Our children, but one that is not prayed for by most. It is the grace to be able to see yourself, your soul as We see it. If you pray for this grace, to be given you from Me, to know yourself as We know you, it will be given you, when We know it is the right time for you to have it. In doing this, you will see the state of your soul, the good and the bad of how the Father sees. You will know what you need to confess and repent of and you are then given the option of doing so. You will be given the grace to be able to come back to the loving arms of the Father Who created you.

October 17 (Feast — St. Ignatius of Antioch, Bishop)
Gift of Mercy

(Holy Spirit speaks) My dear children, I would like to continue with this great grace of love. To see yourself, thereby making the best examination of conscience ever, with My help, you will receive this grace, this gift of Mercy, of the Father's Love, as He shows you what could be in His Justice, if there is no contrition, no repentance. This truly is a great gift and is given to those who seek it now. Then when it is felt the soul is ready to receive this gift, it will be given. It is a gift that then should be shared with others and lived out in its entire completion and in the fullness of time. This is not to say to let others know your sins; no, this is a gift to share in the sense that others should know they too can pray for this grace. I, the Holy Spirit of the Father and the Son, blow graces where I will and enlighten minds and consciences. Come now and pray to be able to be completely in this grace and in the State of Sanctifying Grace, which is what happens to a soul when it has come back to the Father.

October 18 (Feast — St. Luke, Evangelist)
What Jesus Seeks

(Jesus speaks) My beloved children, you must try to die to self, to that self-centered ego, to pride. Do this every day. When you question Me and My Will for you, in anything I ask of you or plan for you, this is part of selfishness and looking to self instead of to Me. I carried My Cross laden with sins, your sins included. Please, put all sins on the Cross and leave them there. Obedience and humility is what I seek to see in My children. It is then that a complete trust will develop between you and Me. There then will be love, undying, unconditional love, for Me, for others, and for yourself. When you have completely died to self, you will then see Me in your whole being and others will see My Light, more clearly, shining through you.

October 19 (Ss. Isaac Joques & John de Brebeuf and Companions) Special Place in Your Heart

(**Jesus speaks**) My beloved children, if you would always remain in Us, you would have love and become love. Look deep within your hearts, My loved ones, and find me, find My Mother. When you seek Me out, you will find Me. It is not very difficult, as I continue to seek you out always. Now, close your eyes and withdraw to that special place in your heart that is **MINE and there I am.** You have found **LOVE!** If you as yet have not made a special place for Us in your hearts, your souls, My Love urges you NOW to consider doing this. If you cannot because of obstacles, please pray, My little ones, for this grace.

October 20 (Feast — St. Paul of the Cross) Special Gifts

(**Jesus speaks**) Beloved children of My Heart, each of you have received special gifts just for yourself, fashioned and molded by Him, your Creator, as He knows you need. When you allow your hearts to control your senses and your minds, you will see with the eyes of your hearts what it is We have given each of you, from the beginning of time and how you should be handling these gifts that each of you has received from the Father. It is now your responsibility to respond to these gifts if you wish, for the greatest of gifts given is **LOVE!**

October 21   Help to Grow in Holiness

(**Mary speaks**) Precious children of My Immaculate Heart, I am here to help each of you who want to grow in holiness and virtue. I am the Queen of all Virtues, Mother of all. Pray from the heart more for the virtues you need. Ask the Holy Spirit to guide you in this and to help you overcome your faults. I am with you to help in this. I am here as well, to help in the renewal of the family and the Church. I cannot do this alone. I need your help, my loved ones. Pray and give me your prayers, so we can defeat the adversary, who is trying to stop my plan for this renewal in your hearts, in your families and in the church.

October 22   Listen and Learn

(**Jesus speaks**) Children of My Sacred and Merciful Heart, learn from Me. Learn from My Mother. In your mother Mary, you have the master teacher of all time, especially in the virtues, Our Virtues. Listen to her as she leads you to Me and to your eternal happiness and peace. Learn from My Joseph. Listen to your Angels. They want so much to help you in this journey back to Us. Then little ones, dialogue, talk with Me and to Me.

October 23   (Feast — St. John Capistrano)
Being One with God

(**Jesus speaks**) My loved little ones, you are to listen always and most attentively to the Holy Spirit, who, with Mary the Immaculate One, will be instructing and guiding each of you. There should no longer exist within you guile, ego, jealousy, resentments, anger and pride. These belong to Satan. You must have Mary's humility, gentleness, joy, hope, faith, unconditional love, complete trust and abandonment to Me. You will then know My Wisdom and much will be revealed to your hearts. Your hearts will no longer be yours but Mine. We will then be as one, think as one, love as one, trust as one; pray, praise, thank, adore as one, the Almighty One; The Father.

October 24 (Feast – St. Anthony Claret, Bishop)
Path to Holiness

(**Mary speaks**) My dear ones, as you continue your path to holiness, to sanctity and to complete, absolute submission to His Will, it will not always be an easy way, but one that will hold for you, who decide to travel it, a glorious rainbow at the end of the journey, leading to His Divine Will. Children, it would be so easy if you were just to be "OUR CHILDREN" in all humility, trust faith and obedience. But, to my great dismay, some decide to go with what the world is offering, the allurements of the moment, the monetary successes, the prestige of being somebody, or so they think, in the eyes of the world. Children, you have forgotten that the first and foremost One to please, to satisfy, to honor, is your Creator, your God, Who knows all, sees all and allows all to happen; the bad with the good.

October 25 Continuing on Path to Holiness

(**Jesus speaks**) Dearest of My Sacred and Merciful Heart, when you love one another unselfishly, thinking of the other above yourself and wanting to please only the other above your feelings and paying no heed to what others may be saying to discourage you, you will then be making inroads into My Heart, into My very Being and into becoming another Me. I invite you, dear ones, you the humble and obedient of heart, to continue to walk in My Light and under the protection of your Mother Mary's Mantle. Be this My Light, for those who are hard and stubborn of heart. You may have to do this to the point of much sacrifice to your own comfort. I cannot penetrate a heart who refuses to acknowledge it could be wrong: one that cannot admit its own sinfulness. Reconcile I beg you, with Me and with Your loved ones, with yourself and get back on the path that leads to Eternal light, happiness and **to holiness.**

October 26 Fruits of Virtue

(**Jesus speaks**) My beloved children, the outcome of prayer and obedience is **holiness.** The fruits of virtue are born by the spirit of those who dwell in the Garden of My Father's Will. Here all is peaceful and each action is fruitful. Here, the effect of your response is completely united to My Heart and the heart of My Mother. This is able to affect the lives of all Our children, who are in need of My mercy. Children, to have a holy righteousness sounds simple, but yet it is so hard, because of your natures and the evil that persists in the world and the deception of the "righteous." This can be overcome only with My help. Call on Me, on the Holy Spirit, on your Immaculate Mother, Mary, on your blessed St. Joseph, your angels and saints. All of Heaven wants to help you succeed in this quest for holiness and for the virtues you need. We are here to help you in the battle against the deception of the evil the world wants you to have and wants you to live.

October 27 No Other Way

(St. Terese, Little Flower speaks) My friends, there is no other way to perfection except through simplicity, purity and living with a humble heart, when one wishes to serve **the Beloved One**. The tiring things we do every day in the life of routine and service while on earth, are powerful opportunities to build a mighty edifice of love for our dearest God. The Son, Who loved us to His Death and obeyed His Father in all ways, has shown us how to unite our present situations to His suffering. Dear ones, the ability to be little and humble in the eyes of each other, will bring freedom and true joy to your hearts. Your hearts, little ones of Jesus, is where you will find everything you need.

October 28 (Feast — Ss. Simon and Jude)
Exercise in Virtue

(Jesus speaks) My little children, it is most necessary to live in an environment of gratitude, as this leads to greater humility. Within each one of you lie the seeds of virtue, which only needs to be desired through prayer and exercised with diligence and patience. Please, My beloved ones, continue to seek humility and simplicity. There is something else each of you should know. It is only My Precious Blood that will save you and *your will* to be saved. When you pray, "take all that I am and have and do with it as You will," it is then that **I Will** you to be united with Me, through this commitment of yourself in special ways: ways which will unfold as I know will be best for you and when it is best for you. Pray for the virtues that you will need to help you in your daily walk.

October 29 Learn From Mary

(**Mary speaks**) My dear little ones, without virtue it is difficult to have mercy and love. Continue to pray to the Holy Spirit for my virtues and my spirit to be yours. My patience with my children is endless. This is what I would like you to learn from me: my patience, my humility, my obedience and my charity. I would like you to pray to imitate these virtues of mine. When you pray for perseverance in humility, obedience, charity and love, know you will be given this, according to His Will for you. Also, know then, much will be asked of you as well.

October 30 Enemy of Virtue

(**Jesus speaks**) My beloved children, flattery, pats on the back are not lessons in humility and dying to self. This adds to pride and pride is contrary to humility. Pride is a complete contradiction of humility, charity and obedience. Pride is one of your greatest enemies. Heed these words of Mine. To overcome the enemy of your soul and its walk towards holiness, learn the lessons My Mother has been teaching for so long. Work on it every day. Take it into your heart and then pray. Pray the Chaplet of Humility every day, along with the Chaplet of Divine Mercy, along with the Holy Rosary. Oh the graces, my beloved ones, you will receive from doing this and how more like My Heart your heart will become.

October 31   Living Christ-like

(**Jesus speaks**) My loved ones, you are created to live My life in all Its dimensions. You are created to receive the eternal rewards earned by My Passion, Death and Resurrection. All the graces you need are here for the asking. These graces are yours for the taking and will be given in an over-abundance, as you repeatedly turn to Us, in complete trust. The joy you will have in living in this way will further convince you to persevere.

Return Love to *"Love"*

NOVEMBER

Being Prepared –
Holy Souls – Thanksgiving

"I will give thanks to You, O Lord, with all my heart, (for You have heard the words of my mouth;) in the presence of the angels I will sing Your praise; I will worship at Your holy temple and give thanks to Your Name. Because of Your kindness and Your truth; for You have made great above all things, Your name and Your promise." (Psalm 138:1-3)

This month you are being asked to meditate on being spiritually prepared in your hearts, minds and souls for whatever the Heavenly Father Wills for you at any one given time, whether it be to help your neighbor, yourself, or having your soul in the state of grace at all times. You are being asked to praise and thank Him for everything in your lives, the good as well as with what you may see as the bad or inconvenient. November is also dedicated to souls, not only the souls in Purgatory, but to all souls, living and dead.

At every opportunity, try to shut out the distractions from the world, by drawing yourself into that secret place which is reserved just for Him. Wherever a soul is, He is, if invited. He should be at the center of each person's being, but because of distractions, it is hard to find Him at times. When you withdraw into that calm area within yourself, that belongs to Him alone, you will have found the Kingdom within, because He is there. Then your real life begins, because you are home.

Our Blessed Mother has said, *"Souls are precious to me, to My Son, Jesus. We want all to be saved. Please, little ones continue to pray, to be in His Love, to invoke His Mercy and my mercy. We intercede before the Throne of the Most High God for all your intentions, at all times and for all the intentions of holy souls who pray for Our intentions. Your prayers, sacrifices, fasting and good works are always being united with my prayers, for the salvation of souls, when given to me and for the conversion of the many We pray for. My prayers are always united with those of Jesus. The Father refuses the Son nothing, as My Son refuses me nothing."*

Mary had this further to say about souls: *"My children, to be in the state of grace is a treasure, because of what the soul becomes in the sight of God. Being in the State of Sanctifying Grace, you become so bright that Angels sing out in loud voices, 'Glory to God in the highest,' joining your soul voices with theirs, in praise of God. Your souls become so elevated that, if you could see with your human eyes, what the eyes of your heart and soul sees, you would know how pleasing you have become to the Holy Trinity. All of Heaven sings in unison with you, as your soul soars to heavenly heights."*

Reflection for the Month:

Jesus has a parable for us: "Dear ones, an instrument is a lowly, plain tool picked up by the Potter, in order to work with the clay, while it is soft and pliable. Many such tools are needed to help form and mold the many clay pots in the Master's shop. Great heat is applied to the lowly containers. They are fired for just the right amount of time to obtain the proper glaze each one needs. These vessels are ornaments at the table of the Master, which serve to nourish those who are invited to the Banquet. My Father and I are preparing the greatest Banquet in the history of Our people. Many vessels are needed to hold the nourishment for Our people starving for the Bread of Life, the Water of Grace and the Meat of Truth. Children, the Kingdom of God is worth fighting for and it is worth praying for. Some of you will see My Second Coming among you in the New Era of Peace. The time spent here, My beloved ones, when you serve the Master, is a mere second on the clock of Eternal Love. The joy of serving the Master overcomes all fatigue, all thoughts of other plans and in order to please Me, the Master, the soul will wait in silent patience to be available for the least desire of her Beloved."

Prayer

I praise and thank you Heavenly Father for all the graces and blessings which you are bestowing on me at all times. Thank you for being my Father, for creating me and for loving my soul as You do. I give praise and thanksgiving for all of your creation, the work of Your Hands. Thank you for everything. Amen.

Resolution

With Your help, Heavenly Father, I will always be prepared for any eventuality that You may allow to happen in my life. I will pray for all holy souls, both living and dead. I will praise and thank you for everything, even the sadness that may occur in my life at any time.

Meditations for November

Being Prepared – Holy Souls – Thanksgiving

"At that moment Jesus rejoiced in the Holy Spirit and said: 'I offer you praise, O Father, Lord of heaven and earth, because what you have hidden from the learned and the clever you have revealed to the merest of children.'"
(Luke 10:21)

November 1   (Feast of All Saints) Souls as the Goal

(**Jesus speaks**) My dearest children, much knowledge is given to a soul showing it what to do to remain in the state of grace. This is most valuable for your salvation. When you know and are shown your soul as the Father sees it, this grace will prove invaluable. The focus is always to be on Me, on your trust in Me, **with souls as your goal.** You must now complete the dying to your old selves and things the world has to offer. This will come through faith and wisdom, from the Wisdom of Faith. Pray continuously for these graces to be complete in you. This will build a solid fortress in your souls and the souls of others, of truth, love and mercy, all through this Wisdom of Faith.

November 2   (Feast of All Souls)
                Words of Encouragement

(**Jesus speaks**) Dearest children, I encourage all of you to increased prayer, frequent confession, and reparation to Our

Hearts, daily Mass and Communion, daily visits to Me in the Blessed Sacrament if you can, according to your state in life. My Words in Holy Scripture are to be lived now and always. I encourage you to know what is written in the Holy Bible, in the Catholic Catechism and in those letters and encyclicals of Our beloved Popes. Most important is to live these words, as well as living in My Will, through My Divine Mercy. Teach it! Show it! Bring it to all My children, for the good of more souls.

November 3   (Feast — St. Martin de Porres)
               Need to Prepare

(**Mary speaks**) Dearest little ones, there is no better way to prepare for anything, for these times you live in, other than by prayer and penance and fasting. Please renew your efforts in this. I am here to help you. Can you give up some of the many trivial and seemingly important little goodies and favors you grant to yourself constantly? There are many opportunities to receive graces that are being offered you. There will be many opportunities for conversions. The time foretold in Scripture is about to unfold. The Holy Spirit will pour out innumerable gifts and graces upon the world. These must be accepted, guarded and nurtured, as the amount of evil increases in the world.

November 4   (Feast — St. Charles Borromeo)
               Be Watchful

(**Mary speaks**) My beloved children, more than ever before, you must be wary of taking the wrong turns in your lives. There will be many who will sound so convincing now, in their deceit, which comes from the adversary, that you need to be ever watchful and in prayer. Only through grace and being bound by the Light of Truth and in total union with Our Hearts (your total giving of all to Us, in complete, trustful consecration to Jesus' Sacred Heart through My Immaculate Heart) will you be able to be strong in the face of any and all trials that face you on a daily basis.

November 5   Eyes of Heart and Mind

(**Mary speaks**) My children, the Gospel from St. Luke (Luke 10:17-24) refers to what **is important** and what **is not** for each of you in your lives. Miracles are performed daily in Jesus' Name on earth and in the heavens, but what outweighs the miracle is the knowledge that eyes are being opened to Him, Who is the only Way, Truth and Life one will ever need. When the eyes of your hearts and minds are opened, you then gladly and willingly receive Jesus and His Love, completely, into your very beings. You are then transformed by His Holy Spirit. You then become one with Him fully and He with you. You begin to put on the mind and Heart of Christ as was always intended.

November 6   Helping Souls on Journey

(**Jesus speaks**) My littlest ones, it is important for you to help Me, help other souls on their journey to salvation. Increasing holiness in your life through graces given will help in the preparation for the salvation of your soul and the souls of others. Souls, yours and your neighbors, must be your goal always. Please read and meditate on Psalm 51. I will create clean hearts in those who wish to have one, a heart that will belong to Me alone, a soul purified to a degree of being ready for anything; either to come to Me for all Eternity, or to stay and help Me in My cause for souls.

November 7   The Triangle

(**Jesus speaks**) Little children please remember **"The Triangle": God** at the top (the focal point). In one corner of the triangle is your neighbor — everyone (your families and all those in the world). In the other corner is you. All souls are important, as are the souls in Purgatory. When you do not step out of this Triangle, you cannot be centered on self, because your **FOCUS** is first on ME, your God, then on your **Neighbor,** and then on **Yourself.** I can work miracles in anyone who will remember this. I am then completely and wholly One with you and your 'self' is no longer your prime concern and focus.

November 8   Spiritual Preparation

(**Jesus speaks**) Dearest children of My Sacred Heart, your spiritual preparation must be permanent and like a "Rock" to the point that you cannot be touched, influenced or moved by anything or anyone, except by Myself or by My Mother. Do not let anything disturb your peace or to re-focus your attention from Me and My Will for you. Continue to pray My Chaplet of Divine Mercy, My Mother's Rosary, as often as you can, for souls, giving these prayers to Us to use where We know they are needed most and for whom they are needed at that moment. One day you will know how important this has been when you see the souls you have helped by your prayers. If you knew how just one more Rosary or Chaplet said could change or alter an event, you would be praying all the time. Please Pray.

November 9   (Feast – Dedication of Lateran Basilica in Rome) Salvation of Souls

(**Mary speaks**) My dearest little ones, come now, to be with Us, in the silence of your hearts, in front of the Blessed Sacrament, or in the privacy of your homes and you will know from what will be given to your hearts, the meaning of Our Words to you. Those of you who are being called by the Father, in His perfect plan for all His children, are to work diligently for the salvation of your soul, as if this was to be the very hour of your coming into His Presence. You will know in that instant whether you deserve to come immediately into Eternal Life, into His Presence forever or not. You will know in that instant and in His Mercy, to ask for forgiveness, or to refuse His love and mercy forever.

November 10   (Feast – St. Leo the Great, Pope/Doctor) Take Care of Your Soul

(**Mary speaks**) My beloved ones, take care of your souls, as you take care of your bodies. Give them to me. Give all of you, to me, to care for, as I then have an obligation, as your mother, to see to it you stay on the right path and take the right steps to insure your holiness. I will help insure the salvation of your souls. Am I not your Mother? If I am and you recognize me as such, COME, RUN, DO NOT CRAWL OR

WALK, BUT RUN, into my loving arms and heart, to feel the security and love of this mother who wants you for God, for all Eternity. **I am yours. Won't you be mine?**

November 11 (Feast — St. Martin of Tours, Bishop)
Salvation Won

(**Jesus speaks**) My beloved children, think with your hearts and not with your minds, first. Listen with your hearts and not with your ears, first. It would be much better to stop listening to so many, especially where you allow confusion and anxiety to work on you. Discern all. Turn always to My Holy Spirit, to Mary, to your Angels and Saints. They are all there to help your soul on its journey toward salvation, to its goal, the salvation I won for you by My Death and Resurrection.

November 12 (Feast — St. Josaphat, Bishop)
Food For the Soul

(**Jesus speaks**) My beloved little ones, it is so difficult, almost impossible, for Me to come to a heart, a soul who is always going, going, and doing, doing. The soul cannot find the time to be with Me wholly and completely, as I wish it to be, when it is not focused. When the soul is doing, doing, it does not have peace. Peace is found being with Me in the silence of your hearts, in My Presence and in the quiet of My Love. This is food for your interior life. It is as necessary as the air you breathe, to be one in heart, mind and soul with Me, your God. This is what one needs and should always desire this. In this way I am able to serve you, to nourish you with the graces and blessings you need to be able to go back into the world, into a world that has no idea of what peace, love and mercy are all about.

November 13 (Feast – St. Frances Cabrini) Mary's Responsibility

(**Mary speaks**) Dearest children of mine, My Son gave me a great responsibility from His Sacrificial Altar, the Cross, when He gave you to Me, to care for, to help in the salvation of your souls, as His co-redeemer, bringing all of you and those lost souls to Him, who have wandered far from Him over the years. These are decisive years, my children. Why are you not listening to My Son Jesus, as He has been teaching, through His Scriptures and through the various vehicles He has used through the years? Jesus has been trying to show you how to live and how to come back to Him, to the Father through Him. He has tried to show you how each of you can be Saints one day in Heaven, as was always planned by the Almighty One, the Father of all.

November 14 What Is To Come

(**Jesus speaks**) My beloved children, you await the coming of many events, yet those events that are now present to you, the daily events, you pay no heed to. You do not see how you can make the difference between the life and death of your world. Do not look for "signs." The signs are there among you. So much has been given you to help you prepare your souls. Will you open the eyes of your hearts to see all of what has been given you for so long? All blessings and graces on those who are now saying "yes" to what I am suggesting to their hearts.

November 15 (Feast — St. Albert the Great,
Bishop/Doctor) Anti-Christ

(**Jesus speaks**) Dear children, some of you look for and speculate on the "Anti-Christ." You wonder who this will be and when he is to come. Have you looked recently within yourselves to see what is anti-Christ? Do you not see what is anti-Christ? Do you not realize that all you do that is against My Commandments, against Our Will and wish for you, IS anti-Christ? When you sin, even the slightest, it is anti-Christ. Anti means to go against, to do something contrary to good. Could this be the evil you are anticipating coming among you? If it is, would you not say that anti-Christ is here and now?

November 16 (Ss. Margaret of Scotland & Gertrude the
Great) Within Hearts, Lives and Attitudes

(**Jesus speaks**) Children, yes, there will come a person who will be called the Anti-Christ. In the waiting for this person, I would suggest you do something about the anti-Christ within your hearts, your lives, your attitudes, and your families. If you can overcome this "ANTI" hurdle, you then would have nothing to fear from the person — Anti-Christ. Your trust, your faith, your virtues would be complete and you could cope with anything and everything the Father is to allow in His world. If you would only come to Me you would be in My peace and in My Heart, surrounded by floods of mercy and love, which come from this Heart.

November 17 (Feast – St. Elizabeth of Hungary)
           Work for Souls

(**Jesus speaks**) My beloved children, as in the book of Isaiah, chapter 30, my children still pay Me no heed as in the time of Isaiah. Help them, My little ones. Please pray with Me to the Father for the many who have strayed from My Sheepfold. Pray that all will accept the graces and mercy being offered them. Work unceasingly for the conversion of sinners. Bring Me the souls that are most difficult and the most impossible to convert. Loved ones, as long as one continues to live a life of competition, anger and bitterness, selfishness and impatience, Satan will have his way with that soul. It is not until that way is broken and the pieces of your life reassembled by Me, through Our Holy Spirit, that a life begins to be lived, according to the Creator's plan for it. Until then, the soul cannot find Me or My Way, because it is drowning in illusion, blinded by the false promises of the world.

November 18 (Dedication of Basilicas of Apostles Peter
           and Paul) Guiding Lights and Beacons

(**Mary speaks**) Dearest of My Immaculate Heart, when you are spiritually prepared in your whole being, you will then see the Reign of Our Hearts, the Triumph of My Immaculate Heart with the Reign of the Sacred Heart of My Son, Jesus. Always be in readiness for no one knows the hour of your destiny, when it will be the time of your fulfillment of God's plan for you in this pilgrimage on earth. Pray to always be in the state of grace. The following you could call

"Spiritual To Do's" from your heavenly mother: *Please try to go to Mass and Communion daily; Go to confession regularly, monthly or even weekly; Keep your souls in the state of grace; Have Perpetual Adoration when possible; Pray your priests will see the value of being in the Real Presence of My Son, through adoration. Vigils of prayer are most important.*

November 19   Important Feast Days

(**Mary speaks**) My beautiful children, there should be much preparation of the heart before important feast days. Much prayer and fasting is recommended. Perhaps a Novena before, as well. This can be done individually or in community. I, your mother, want to form many prayer communities, so those in these communities will be able to withstand all that is to come. They then will be guiding lights to others, a beacon for those who are in need spiritually. There must be a change in hearts. It is the eleventh hour of grace and of mercy; that is why it is imperative to increase prayer. You must live each day as if it were your last.

November 20   Listen – Live – Act

(**Jesus speaks**) Children of My Heart, it is time to stop doing other things that may take you away from Me. Act on what We are telling you for your own spiritual preparedness. You will then be a light for those who will need you and will seek you out in their needs. Please listen to the spirit of truth, only. You must not be busy about anything other than what My Mother and I have requested of you. Bring your soul and other souls to Me, thereby helping Us in the harvest of souls in this time of mercy, all through My Mercy. Mercy is all the virtues and living them in My Perfect Will for you.

November 21   Communion with Jesus

(Mary speaks) My beloved children, discover that today nothing is as important for you as time spent in greater communion with My Son and His desires and words for you. This now is paramount in your preparation. What joy the soul has who knows me and knows My Son. It pleases Us to do everything for that soul. Continue to always pray for conversions, for sinners and for those who seem not to want to accept Jesus. You do well to pray continuous Rosaries and Chaplets of Mercy for souls who seem lost and those who may be on the brink of perdition. Help Us help them, your brothers and sisters. Continue to strive each day for holiness and to pray for souls. I love you so tenderly.

November 22   (Feast – St. Cecilia) Pearls of Grace

(Mary speaks) Dearest children of My Heart, each of your souls have special graces, pearls of grace that are for you alone and no one else. Your soul matures spiritually according to your faith and your complete trust in Him. Souls are like small children and are to be handled gently and carefully so as not to harm their progress of growth. It takes a short time for some and others, a much longer time, for this progress to take place. The Father has planned this time span before the world began. When a soul has reached this certain spiritual maturity, by grace, the little pearls of grace given to that soul become most precious and valuable in Our safe keeping, in Our store of treasures.

November 23 (St. Clement I, Columban, Bl. Miquel Pro) Soul's Free Will

(**Mary speaks**) Dear ones, each soul has been given a free will, this too being a pearl of grace. If handled according to the plan of the Heavenly Father, the soul will unite itself more readily to His Will, which is the ultimate goal for all souls: a complete unity with Him in His Will. This is when the soul no longer cares to exercise his free will, but rather returns his will to the Giver, the Creator. Plan now to give Us your hearts and souls in a pure package, suitable for the King of Kings, the God of the Universe.

November 24 (Feast — St. Andrew Dung-Lac and Companions) Do Not Worry About Tomorrow

(**Jesus speaks**) My beloved children, you are not to trouble over what tomorrow will bring. Work on what We have planned for you TODAY. As you work and live each day as I direct, as I Will, you will find the tomorrow's will come easily and unfold in mysterious and wonderful ways. Focus on Me, on My love, on My mercy and how your prayers and your love can help this aching world of yours. There is a darkness of the soul that can invade you and then choices will seem more difficult. It is then to be completely focused on My Face and all you know to be true and holy.

November 25   See With Eyes of Heart/Soul

(**Mary speaks**) My dear, dear children, each time you feel panic begin to invade your being, stop! Refocus on My Son and Myself. Ask to be reunited to Our Hearts and be allowed to concentrate again on truth and the reality of all that is. There are many souls who miss what the Father intended for it and still intends for all souls. As Scripture has said: "they have eyes, but do not see, they have ears but do not hear." (Matt. 13:15) They see only what their minds, eyes, feelings tell them and this is usually from the world. Once you have learned the secret to listen and see with the heart, your soul will still see and hear what is about them, but you are now listening and seeing with your hearts.

November 26   Miracles and Transformation Happen

(**Mary speaks**) Dearest ones of My Immaculate Heart, when a soul is in the state of sanctifying grace, it is likened to a radiant jewel and it has gained the Kingdom here on earth. A soul in the state of sanctifying grace is a place where the Most Holy Trinity wants to dwell at all times. This soul is then Their special delight because They can come freely, through me, into my garden, in your soul and rest. This gives a soul much peace, joy and happiness which is not describable. In the silence of your hearts, souls, miracles happen, transformations occur, changes take place and grace takes hold of you in your interior castle, the soul.

November 27 Preparing for Heaven

(**St. Francis of Assisi speaks**) Brothers and sisters, praying to be in Heaven is something each of you should strive
for and you should be preparing for this at the very outset of
your lives on earth. You will find, as we have who are now in
our heavenly home, that your journey, your pilgrimage on
earth is but a short distance to what you will spend in eternity
with all of us. Also know that when you see Jesus' mother,
Mary, you see Him. You will see truth. You will see light.
You will see the way to Him, to the life here He wishes for
your preparation to the eternal life that He wants for all of
you in Heaven with Them and with us.

November 28 Beloved Departed

(**Jesus speaks**) My beloved ones, many of your loved rela-
tives, friends for whom you have prayed for so long, through
Me, to the Father, are now basking in the Eternal, Heavenly
Light, which never dims or goes out. Because of your prayers,
many of these souls, whom you have prayed in such earnest
for, are now enjoying eternal bliss with Us in Heaven. They
will be eternally grateful for your prayers and will now be
praying for each of you, for your safe journey, when the Father calls you to this Eternal Light with Us.

November 29 Choices

(**Jesus speaks**) Children of My Sacred Heart, please pray
to understand and to know what it is you are being called to
do. It is your choice whether or not to change, to see My

Light or not, to follow Me or not, My dear ones. All of these things are your choices. How you choose will determine your fate and your future. It would be wise to remember to live today as you are being led, leaving the tomorrows to Me, as I have planned for you. Then put the yesterdays where they belong, in the past. Do not open yesterday's door. Open only today's door, the door that leads to Me, to your joy and the fulfillment of your every need.

November 30   (Feast – St. Andrew, Apostle) Giving Glory
to the Trinity

(**Jesus speaks**) Loved ones of My Merciful Heart, each time you are obedient, each time you defer to the Will of the Father, each time you graciously agree to wait just a little longer for His Will to be done in your life, The Trinity of God is given much glory, honor and praise. Much faith is needed to justify the many that will return to Us at the very last moment. Please pray now, with Us, and always, for the Coming of the Kingdom. **The salvation of the entire world is in the hands of those who pray.** This is the central thought in all Our prayer requests. Prepare yourselves each moment of the day to be emptied more totally and filled more completely with grace and peace and strength.

DECEMBER

New Beginnings – Thoughts to Ponder

> "The angel went on to say to her: 'Do not fear, Mary. You have found favor with God. You shall conceive and bear a son and give Him the name Jesus. Great will be His dignity and he will be called Son of the Most High. The Lord God will give Him the throne of David his father. He will rule over the house of Jacob forever and His reign will be without end.'" (Luke 1:30-34)

This is a month to review our year and to think about what has transpired in our lives. It is a good time to truly "ponder things" as Mary did, to see what the past held and what God will possibly have in store for us as a "New Beginning" in the coming year.

Reflection for the Month:

Jesus has much for us to reflect on for the month as well as the months to come: "My beloved children, in this holy month you will be celebrating a most important feast in My Church. This feast not only honors My Beloved Virgin Mother in Her Immaculate Conception, but pays honor and glory to the Triune God for all They have done in and through this most blessed and august Queen of Heaven and Earth. She it is, who is the favored daughter of the Most High, God the Father; She it is, who is the mother of the Son: She it is, who is favored as the Spouse of Our Holy Spirit. She is and always will be Queen of Heaven and Earth and a mother to all Our children.

"Soon you will celebrate, once again, My First Coming among you. Please children, so beloved of My Heart, remember what you are celebrating and why, as you draw near to the day of My birth, a date given you by My Church. Join with all of heaven in praise and thanksgiving to Our Father in Heaven, for having given you this special gift. Think now how to best thank Him and Me and Our Holy Spirit and what you can give Us in return. This is a very special time of year. Many graces will be given when hearts are put in Our Hands and are ready to receive what the Triune God and the Holy Family wishes to give, to bestow on each of you, Our children.

"Also, my loved ones, remember, that earth must be tilled and turned in order to renew it; to refresh it. The soil must be aerated for proper drainage. Each seedling will yield a rich abundance for the time of reaping the harvest. My children of promise, you will receive the fruits of this planting and be nourished for all time to come."

Prayer

Heavenly Father, graciously accept our family which we dedicate and consecrated to You and to The Holy Family. Please guard, protect and keep it in holy fear, peace and in the harmony of Your love. May we, by conforming ourselves to Your Holy Family, attain eternal happiness one day. Visit our home and bless it and keep it safe from the snares of the enemy. Keep us in holiness. We ask all this through Jesus Christ our Lord. Amen.

Resolution

Timely thought for any time of year (replaces resolution for month): The Blessed Mother had given to a chosen soul at one time this beautiful prayer (this is to be done just before the Consecration at the Mass, when Jesus then becomes wholly present to us, Body, Blood, Soul and Divinity) "Dear ones, ask me, your mother, to gather up all the souls of those that are present at the Mass (where you are in attendance) and those of your loved ones, plus all those you've given to me, to pray for with you, and for all souls you wish me to intercede for with you, and I will send my angels to gather them all and place them on His Sacrificial Altar, and at the time of the Transubstantiation, I will plead with Him to look with mercy and love on all those I have laid before Him and beg Him to please heal each soul according to its needs and His Will."

Meditations For December

New Beginnings – Thoughts to Ponder

"You know very well that the day of the Lord is coming like a thief in the night. Just when people are saying, 'peace and security,' ruin will fall on them with the suddenness of pains overtaking a woman in labor, and there will be no escape . . . therefore, let us not be asleep like the rest, but awake and sober! Sleepers sleep by night and drunkards drink by night. We who live by day must be alert, putting on faith and love as a breastplate and the hope of salvation as a helmet." (1 Thessalonians 5:2-3,6-8)

December 1   Do All In Charity and Love

(Jesus speaks) My beloved children, I urge you not to worry, for one second, about anything. Look forward to serving Me, your brothers and sisters and to helping them return to My Body through My Sacraments; through love and forgiveness. The Day of the Lord is upon all of you, My dear children. Do everything now in love, in charity, in wisdom and always in My Will. My love knows no bounds. There is a light that will always be there, for those who will to and want to see with the eyes of their hearts.

December 2   Pray For Renewal of Hearts

(Mary speaks) Dear ones of My Immaculate Heart, a new era is about to dawn as it did at the First Pentecost. Pray, loved ones, for this renewal to be in all hearts, as My Triumph will then be complete and Jesus' Sacred Heart will Reign in all hearts, as has been planned. Yours is to wait with much patience, love, perseverance and joy, for the hour of your deliverance. Live and teach the truth of the Gospel. Share with all who will be sent to you, yourself and your knowledge, regardless of who they are. Souls will be crying out for help. Gather all of them into your hearts and give them to me. My children, a New Day of Grace will be dawning for all of you, who will accept it. Your heart, your spirit must be at peace, with and in Us. Then joy and holiness will seep into the spirit, into your hearts and will cancel out, through grace, any negatives that are trying to take over, even the positives that are not from God.

December 3   (Feast — St. Francis Xavier)
                  Brink of New Era

(Mary speaks) Dear children of My Immaculate Heart, today we stand on the brink of a new era, consecrated and committed to the Divine Will of Our Father in Heaven. You, my dear, dear ones, are all so very dear to My Heart. I am so in love with each of you, with the tenderness of a mother's heart. Please know that we are closer together now than we have ever been before. My Son is about to return to earth once again. As I was prepared long ago to bring the Babe into the world the first time in Bethlehem, now the Father sends me once again, to all of you, to help you too prepare to receive Him, your Jesus, your Savior and My Son. The Holy Spirit will fill you with the necessary love and strength in order that you may greet Him on that glorious day. For now, prepare your hearts to celebrate, once again, His glorious coming at Christmas time.

December 4   (Feast — St. John Damascene)
Presence of Jesus and Mary

(**Mary speaks**) Dearest ones of My Heart, you whose hearts are open to My Son, Jesus, as Savior and King and open to me, your mother, the mother of Jesus, will always be made aware of Our Presence, Our guidance, Our protection and Our closeness. With this openness there is that oneness that is being established and will never be withdrawn until the day when you are in Heaven with Us for all of Eternity. If you feel your lives on earth are long, when you enter into Eternity, to be there forever, you will know how foolish some of your thinking was on earth, as to time and space. Pray always to be holy, to be a saint, to be with Us in Heaven, as was always planned.

December 5   Good Will Surround You

(**Jesus speaks**) My loved little ones, with prayer, sacrifice, fasting and uniting all with Us, nothing is ever lost. This can achieve the impossible and conquer much. The outcome of the battle between good and evil depends on you. We need you. We depend on you, our beloved ones, to help in this important mission for souls and for defeating evil with good. When good surrounds you, you will know that evil has been conquered; you will know that the Reign of My Sacred Heart along with the Triumph of Mary's Immaculate Heart will be complete. **"My love reigns in suffering. It triumphs in humility and It rejoices in unity."**

December 6   (Feast — St. Nicholas, Bishop)
Yourself as Gift

(**Jesus speaks**) Dear ones of My Merciful Heart, at this holy time of year, be prepared in holiness to receive what We wish to give you. Then in true humility, give Us something of yourselves in return, as gift. Give Us your hearts, your souls, your wills. Give Us your entire self. You will, as you do this, see God. You will become Christ-like and you will walk in holiness with Mary your Immaculate Mother and with Joseph, her most chaste spouse. You will walk with them up that road that leads to the gate of heaven, here on earth and for all eternity.

December 7   (Feast — St. Ambrose, Bishop/Doctor)
New Beginning

(**Jesus speaks**) Let every morning, My dearest children, be a new beginning of your preparation for the Will of My Father. Thank Him first and then listen for His whisperings of love. Seek now to build up the secret well of grace and strength deep within yourself so you can dip into this refreshing treasure and be renewed and strengthened. Stay always in the protection and refuge of Our Hearts and under Mary's Mantle of hope, obedience and perseverance. A calm sea must be within you at all times.

December 8 (Feast of Immaculate Conception of Virgin Mary) The Present and the Past

(**Jesus speaks**) Dear ones, My mother and I love you beyond what any words could tell. The future is dependent on love, dearest children. The present is sustained by love and the past is a reflection of the love My Father has given to you, His beloved people. Only love will remain when all is purified. It is a new beginning My children need in order to return to the understanding of Truth as it has always been revealed. Be grateful for each event that develops in your life as it is a means of teaching you more about yourself and exposing your weakness. Trust that there will be a New Day and in this day love will flourish as it once did, in the hearts of man. Everyone will be at peace as it was intended from the beginning of time.

December 9 (Feast — Bl. Juan Diego) For Families

(**Blessed Mother speaks**) My children, at special times during the year, such as Christmas, you should do a consecration together, as a family, doing it in love to His Sacred Heart through My Immaculate Heart. This consecration should be done with a pure heart and with much love. It is so important to be in the state of grace. To make a total consecration of your family to His Sacred Heart through my Immaculate heart is a commitment. Pray much for families as this is where Jesus inspires and instills special graces on the young and on the parents. Keep holiness alive through family prayer and encourage the young to consider the religious life. From these ranks will come the next generation of Saints.

December 10   Come to the Heart of Jesus

(**Jesus speaks**) My precious children, We (the Triune God) want you to know your God loves you very much, unconditionally, no matter what you may think and no matter what the world is trying to tell you. We want you with Us Now and for all eternity. **Come, come into My Heart Now**, through the door of Mary's Immaculate Heart and she will take you by the hand, as only a loving mother knows how to do. She will bring you into that refuge of My Sacred and Merciful Heart where miracles are wrought. Once there, I then prepare you to meet your Creator, the Father of all in Heaven, the Almighty and Glorious One. Yes, dear ones, Heaven can be and is here on Earth. **Find love and you find Me.** You then have found Heaven here on Earth. When you find Me, you will have a taste, a look at what is waiting for you and what it will be like in Eternity with Us.

December 11   (Feast — St. Damascus I, Pope) New Dawn

(**Mary speaks**) Little ones of My Heart, keep holding my hand. Pray with your angels unceasingly. Carry your rosaries, your scapulars always, my precious ones. Use your holy water frequently. Much faith is needed. Faith can be obtained through much prayer. Pray for my gentleness, wisdom and understanding. Have a complete and unalterable trust in Jesus' Sacred and Merciful Heart. Your hope, trust and faith will be rewarded when the New Dawn comes. Then will follow the Triumph of Our Hearts, which will be felt by everyone and light will fill every area of your world with Our love and peace. Please my children, desire to be holy and to be Saints. This is what We want for you.

December 12 (Feast — Our Lady of Guadalupe)
Promises

(**Jesus speaks**) Children of My Loving Heart, it will be Our Love that brings you to a new day soon and to a continued faith in Our promises to you. It will be your faith and trust which will enable Us to lead you to the truth always and to the patience you will need to wait for the fulfillment of Our promises. It will be necessary for you to wait patiently for His Will for each of your lives and for your lives collectively.

December 13 (Feast — St. Lucy)
New Heaven and a New Earth

(**Mary speaks**) Loved children of Ours, stay close to me, little ones, as soon a **new Heaven and a new Earth** are to become a reality. My Angels and Myself are with you always. Bathe yourselves in the waters of grace and forgiveness. Dress yourselves with my virtues and the gifts of the Holy Spirit, my Beloved Spouse. Adorn your heads with rejoicing and sing songs of praise, then give thanks to the Father. Wait in humble service to your brothers and sisters. Rejoice with me for the King of Glory is to be celebrated once again. This King will come again, soon to save you once again. Be ready for His return in Glory. I praise the Father, my Son and Their Spirit in unity with all of Heaven and earth. I am your mother who loves you!

December 14   (Feast – St. John of Cross) Prepare for The Second Coming

(**Jesus speaks**) Dear ones, it is most important you have your hearts ready at all times. Prepare them every morning and evening for My coming again in your midst. My Second Coming is imminent. The Triumph of Mary's Immaculate Heart is soon to come, along with the Reign of My Sacred Heart. Prepare your hearts, NOW, for it is time. Only the Father knows when this will occur. All of Heaven is preparing for it now. Wait and be ready for these events to happen.

December 15   Mother and Queen of The New Advent

(**Mary speaks**) Dearest children, having given birth to the God-Man some 2000 years ago, through the working of the Holy Spirit, my Heavenly Spouse, I have now been asked again, in this time, to take my children by the hand through my heart and lead them into the New Advent, the coming of the year 2000 and beyond. This will be a momentous time as many will be drawn again to My Son, to the Father and to the Holy Spirit. All in unified power (The Holy Trinity) will pronounce the coming of this New Advent. I, the Mother of Mercy, will lead you as the Mother and Queen of the New Advent. I am the New Eve and He, My Son, the New Adam. We ask you, Our children, to please pray with Us for this coming event.

December 16   Leading Gently to Him

(**Mary speaks**) My beloved ones, I have been taking you, all my children, and leading you gently, since Jesus gave you to me, towards His Second Coming among you, His children, as He has promised, as the Father has promised. You are being asked to prepare your hearts and your souls, through a total giving of yourself to Jesus through me, as this is the only way you will be able to travel this road with Us into the new century and beyond. Many things are on the horizon. There is much hope and joy as all of Heaven is preparing with me, their Queen, to present your King once again to the world, to the hearts in which He will rule supreme. His reign is forever and is going to come through My Immaculate Heart, as I am the Immaculate Conception and the Bride of the Holy Spirit.

December 17   Much to Come

(**Mary speaks**) My loved children, so much is yet to come, to happen, before His Second Coming can occur. You will all need to come from the mire into the new. Be watchful. Be prepared. Be in prayer. Be in the state of grace at all times. Be in me and I in you, as I bring Him once more to you my children. Love, peace and joy make the difference. Pray with me always and never let go of my hand, as I will never let go of yours, unless you ask to have this done. Become as that little child now and I will lead you. As your trust grows, so shall your faith. Do all for His honor and glory. Give praise to Our Father Who so loves the world that He will send His only Son again, to save His people and bring all to the completion of this Age. *"The future of all who pray is bright with the Light of Christ, My Son. Be filled with joy,* as We work together for the good of mankind. Be filled with gratitude to the Father for allowing this extended time of Grace."

December 18   Wisdom of the Father

(**God, the Father speaks**) My beloved ones, ask what you will and it will be given, according to what is best for your souls. The souls of My dear faithful ones are a gold gleaming in the Light of My Son, the Christ and Savior I have sent into the world. Only My Wisdom can determine the proper moment for the commencement of My Plans for you and for My universe. You are My creation and I act with the greatest love and mercy to prepare everything and everyone for the return of My Son. It is with great anticipation for His return that I send special signs and wonders to the world. Be filled with longing for Me, My dear ones. Be filled with gratitude for My Love for you and go in the peace of My Will. I AM!

December 19   Decisions

(**Jesus speaks**) My beloved children, I wish to give each of you the grace to be able to decide in your free will, which is a great and loving gift from the Father, to come and follow Me now, TODAY! Lay down all that is not of Me. Turn your backs on the world. NOW. Without Our grace and a complete unity with Us, you will not be able to survive what the world has in store for you. Please, won't you come to Me? I love you and wish you to be Mine, NOW and for all Eternity. Come into My loving arms, into My Heart so I can heal you and give you all the nourishment (grace) you will ever need. I love you and I am waiting. Come!

December 20   True Meaning of the Season

(**Mary speaks**) My dearest little ones, you are all so loved and cherished by me, by My Divine Son, as you prepare your hearts each day now, until the celebration day of Jesus' first coming into your world, for His birth in that lowly stable in Bethlehem, 2000 years ago. Remember to keep your hearts focused on the true meaning of this season and why My Son Jesus, the Son of God, chose to come to all of us as He did, through me, His Blessed Vessel, His Ark, His Immaculate Home. Remember too, and meditate on the overwhelming and unfathomable love of a Father for all His children, to send His only Son, to call us out of darkness, into the light of His grace, mercy and love. This is a very important time for the preparation of your souls.

December 21   (Feast – St. Peter Canisius) Return Love

(**Mary speaks**) Dear ones of My Immaculate Heart, I am Queen of Heaven, Earth and of all hearts who accept me as mother and queen. I come to reaffirm my love for you, a love that burns at all times and yearns for you to return this love, not to me but to My son, Jesus, for Whom all love belongs. My love is His and His love is mine. His love goes out to all of you through and with My Immaculate Heart. **He is Love and I am the Mother of Love.** Won't you in some small portion, return this love for love to Love Himself? We love as only Love can. How can you refuse this your mother's and your Heavenly Queen's invitation? Please accept these my gifts given to you.

December 22 Adoration and Prayer

(**Jesus speaks**) My loved ones, pray for conversions. Pray for your country's leaders. Pray hearts will change and be healed. The next years are very crucial times for souls. Through your efforts of prayer and sacrifice, many souls will be drawn into My mercy to see, live and know merciful love as it is. Come now, please, if you can, as much as two hours a day for adoration and prayer with Me, no matter what else you think important. This is most important for your soul and the souls of the many. **In listening you will be led. In answering you will be protected.**

December 23   (Feast – St. John of Kanty)
Triumph of Two Hearts

(**Jesus speaks**) My beloved ones, please pray as you never have before, for your brothers and sisters in Russia, for their complete conversion. Soon My flower Russia will come once again into My loving Arms. There is hope. As with love and justice, there will be mercy. Peace will reign again and there will be joy in all hearts. Won't you please be Our instruments and vessels of peace, of trust, of obedience, of humility, of charity, of love and of My mercy? My little ones, the Kingdom is about to be revealed for all to see and choose. The Triumph of Our Two Hearts has begun. I call on each one of you to be My beacon and to live My love and My words for all. This is a holy time of year. Come with your gifts to the throne of the Most High, to the Crib in Bethlehem.

December 24   (Vigil of Christmas) Eternal Life

(**Jesus speaks**) My dear children, what better time of year than the night before I came to earth to be among you, the first time. You celebrate My birthday, My first coming tonight and tomorrow. It is time you started preparing for My Second Coming, now as well. Listen now: I am always waiting in hearts, but rarely does one come to be only with Me, to listen to Me, in the silence of that secret place, the home in your hearts that belongs to Me and Me alone. When you enter in and with Me (to My Heart and I to yours) you then allow Me to wholly be in you. You are then realizing a small taste of Eternal life. This is not life as you know it to be. It is a **life completely absorbed in Me.** Your home has always been destined to be with Me. Eternal life is to know God the Father, God the Son and God the Holy Spirit. This is the happiness all will live in Eternity and can live here and now, if completely in My Will, giving all to Me, even your will and your souls. Pray for this grace, My children. Gift Me this holy night with yourself, giving Me the gift I prize most, your whole self, body, soul and will. In this way you then are being prepared for that Second Coming of your Jesus, soon.

December 25   (Birth of Our Lord – Christmas) Praise and Glorias

(**Mary speaks**) Dearest, most precious children of Mine, yes, today belongs to Him but also belongs to you. He came for you, for me, for all people, so we all could enjoy once again the Kingdom of Heaven. Give Him and the Father in Heaven much honor, praise and thanksgiving for all the gifts

He bestows on each of you. Now decide, please, what it is you wish to give Him in return. Are you ready to return love for love to Love? No matter, dear ones, where you have been placed in the plan of the Father, you must now be completely empty of self, so you can be ready to accept in trust, faith, hope and much joy, what it is that will be and is being asked of you. Each of you is a piece in this salvation puzzle of the Father's and in order for the pieces to fit perfectly, you need to be in complete submission and readiness at all times. Our love, Our peace is always with you.

December 26   (Feast – The Holy Family)
              Living Mercy and Love

(**Jesus speaks**) My loved children, when you start to depend on Me, calling on My Divine Mercy, living all My Mother and I have taught through the ages, asking for the grace and the virtues needed to overcome self and your faults, barriers will begin to disappear and changes will take place. You will start to see with your heart and soul — ME, and will want nothing then but to please Me, nothing but to be with Me in Our Divine Will. Only with much prayer, fasting and sacrificing and the following of Me, living in My mercy, showing My mercy to others, to yourself and to Me, your God, can you find yourself then wanting to be in the Light of Divine Will, as the Father had always planned for it to be.

December 27   (Feast – St. John, Apostle/Evangelist)
              Perpetual Adoration

(**Mary speaks**) Dearest ones of My Heart, the plan from the Triune God is to have Perpetual Adoration flourish in all

Our Churches in the world. When this is done many will come, grace will abound and there will be many conversions. When you reach out to the young, to anyone, teach them the great value of devotion to Him in the Eucharist and in Adoration of Him, their God, in the Blessed Sacrament. You then will experience a rise in vocations. Many will return to the Faith because of Perpetual Adoration. Eucharistic Adoration is the life blood for souls. It is He, your God, reaching out to you, His creatures, in His love and mercy, giving Himself to you, in His Real Presence, before you. It is most important all Our children spend as much time as possible with Him.

December 28   (Feast of Holy Innocents)
The Name of Jesus

(**Jesus speaks**) My children, those of you who have been consecrated to Me, through Mary, the Immaculate One, will have to remember this consecration daily from now on and sometimes hourly, as your trials will now become even more so. But, as you resist and call upon your Mother and as you call upon My Name, the Name that dispels demons, **JESUS**, you and I will then be walking the same path and you will have resisted the wiles of Satan. As this is done more frequently, you will truly be strengthening the faith you acquired through your Baptism into My Death and will then start to live in union with My Resurrection.

December 29   (Feast — St. Thomas Becket, Bishop)
The Divine Physician

(**Jesus speaks**) My beloved little ones, put on now the armour of truth. This will be your greatest strength. The truth will set you free on every occasion, little ones. Take refuge in My Truth and be comforted by it when there is no other comfort to be found. I want the best for each of you, My beloved children. The best is when you have found Me, have found My Truth. Do not despair over struggles. Do not allow your peace and calm to be destroyed by anyone. Please unite your sufferings with Mine for the salvation of the world. Be at peace! Now come to Me, your Divine Physician, and I will heal your wounds and dry your tears. For your comfort and consolation follow My ways and acknowledge Me as your Lord and God.

December 30   Increase Your Prayer

(**Jesus speaks**) My dear ones, strengthen yourselves through much prayer and then more prayer. PLEASE TRUST ME. My light will purify the earth. Increase your prayer groups. Reach out to the corners of each of your states, your communities, to make sure prayer is foremost. The Mass is the primary prayer with Holy Communion. Spread My Mercy to all who will accept it. Be My beacon, by taking one day at a time, as I give it to you. There will be no doubt left in your mind as to My Will for you. You will truly find the meaning of the words, TRUST, FAITH AND WILL GAIN THE WISDOM OF FAITH, by listening to Me in the silence of your hearts to My inspiration and to My guidance. Keep joy, peace, love and trust in your hearts at all times. You are loved as only We can love and will be for all eternity. Will you now return love to Love?

December 31 (Feast — St. Sylvester I, Pope)
New Beginnings

(**Mary speaks**) My beloved children, live now as though nothing else existed save Our Presence with all the Angels and Saints, for this is truly living in the Kingdom. Life always continues after a person dies. However, you continue to live and grow and learn and develop in new ways. As you surrender more and more to being deeply committed to God's Will in each step you take, you will discover this. A new day will dawn for all to see who will turn and be faithful to My Son. Please want to return now, to your Father's house. We want to reassure Our children, each of you, of the wonderful, unchangeable love and mercy We have for each of you. We cannot change you or your thinking. Only you can do this for yourselves. We can only suggest what WE know is best for you and for the good of your soul. We cannot interfere with your free will, but We can urge you to reconsider how it works in your life and how love plays a part in this life of yours. There is no room for fear, only for love. Therefore, my dear ones, live love today and for the tomorrows to come.

Prayer Suggestions

The following prayer meditation we present you prior to the suggested prayers, because it is felt that St. John Chrysostom had a wonderfully, inspired and holy insight into what prayer is and should be.

Prayer is the Light of the Spirit
— by St. John Chrysostom, Bishop

"Prayer and converse with God is a supreme good: it is a partnership and union with God. As the eyes of the body are enlightened when they see light, so our spirit, when it is intent on God is illumined by His Infinite Light.

"I do not mean the prayer of outward observance but prayer from the heart, not confined to fixed times or periods, but continuous throughout the day and night.

"Our spirit should be quick to reach out toward God, not only when it is engaged in meditation; at other times also, when it is carrying out its duties, caring for the needy, performing works of charity, giving generously in the service of others. Our spirit should long for God and call Him to mind; so that these works may be seasoned with the salt of God's Love and so make a palatable offering to the Lord of the universe. Throughout the whole of our lives we may enjoy the benefit that comes from prayer, if we devote a great deal of time to it.

"Prayer is the light of the spirit, true knowledge of God, mediating between God and man. The spirit raised up to the heaven, by prayer, clings to God with the utmost tenderness; like a child crying tearfully for its mother, it craves the milk that God provides. It seeks the satisfaction of its own desires and receives gifts outweighing the whole world of nature.

"Prayer stands before God as an honored ambassador. It gives joy to the spirit, peace to the heart. I speak of prayer, not words. It is the longing for God, love too deep for words, a gift not given by man but by God's grace. The apostle Paul says 'We do not know how we are to pray, but the Spirit Himself pleads for us, with inexpressible longings.'

"When the Lord gives this kind of prayer to a man, He gives him riches that cannot be taken away, heavenly food that satisfies the spirit. One who tastes this food is set on fire with an eternal longing for the Lord: his spirit burns as in a fire of the utmost intensity.

"Practice prayer from the beginning. Paint your house with the colors of modesty and humility. Make it radiant with the light of justice. Decorate it with the finest gold leaf of good deeds. Adorn it with the walls and stones of faith and generosity. Crown it with the pinnacle of prayer. In this way, you will be making it a perfect dwelling place for the Lord. You will be able to receive Him as in a splendid palace, and through His Grace, you will already possess Him. His Image will be enthroned in the temple of your spirit."

The Holy Rosary

The message of the Angel Gabriel "Hail Mary..." (or "Rejoice Mary" in the original Greek text) is a message of joy. Since the rose is a symbol of joy the sequence of 150 Hail Mary's by which we honor Mary and beg her intercession, is called the **"Rosary."** We pray 150 because there are 150 Psalms. From the earliest times it was the duty of priests and religious to regularly pray the Psalms. For lay-brothers, who could not read, it was the practice to pray 150 Ave-Maria's instead. During each ten Ave's they would meditate upon a mystery of the Faith. This is how the Rosary in its present form originated.

Usually one prays a third each day: five decades of ten Hail Mary's. On Mondays and Thursdays we pray the five **Joyful Mysteries:**

The Annunciation
The Visitation
The Nativity
The Presentation
The Finding

On Tuesdays and Fridays the five **Sorrowful Mysteries:**

The Agony in The Garden
The Scourging at The Pillar
The Crowning With Thorns
The Carrying of The Cross
The Crucifixion & Death

And on Wednesdays and Saturdays the five **Glorious Mysteries** which are the foundation of Christian life:

> *The Resurrection*
> *The Ascension*
> *The Descent of The Holy Spirit*
> *The Assumption of Mary*
> *The Coronation of Mary*

After announcing the Mystery we begin each decade with the "Our Father" followed by ten "Hail Marys" and at the end of the decade the "Glory Be" in honour of the most Holy Trinity. This is followed by:

> *Oh My Jesus forgive us our sins, save us from the fires of Hell. Lead all souls to heaven most especially those in need of Thy mercy.*

The Litany of Humility

The Litany of Humility (Source: Pieta Prayer Book)

O Jesus, Meek and humble of Heart, hear me....
From the desire of being esteemed....
From the desire of being loved....
From the desire of being extolled....
From the desire of being praised....
From the desire of being consulted....
From the desire of being approved....
"Deliver me, Jesus" (to be said after each of above)

From the fear of being humiliated....
From the fear of being despised....
From the fear of suffering rebukes....
From the fear of being calumniated....
From the fear of being forgotten....
From the fear of being ridiculed....
From the fear of being wronged....
From the fear of being suspected....
"Deliver Me, Jesus" (to be said after each of above)

That others may be loved more than I....

That others may be esteemed more than I....

That in the opinion of the world, others may increase and I may decrease....

That others may be chosen and I set aside....

That others may be praised and I unnoticed....

That others become holier than I, provided that I may become as holy as I should....

"Jesus, grant me the grace to desire it." (to be said after each of the above)

Novena Prayer to Saint Anthony

(Good prayer for conversion.)

Loving Saint Anthony
You always reached out in compassion
to those who had lost their faith.
You were especially concerned
because they had lost access to the
healing words of Jesus found in the
Sacrament of Reconciliation and in

the nourishing presence of Jesus
in the Sacrament of the Eucharist.

Intercede for _____
who has stopped practicing his/her faith.
Reawaken in his/her heart a love
for our Church and the sacraments,
and enkindle in his/her heart a sense
of forgiveness for the ways he/she
might have been hurt by members
of the Church who fell short of the
teaching of Christ.

Finally, St. Anthony, help me to
respond to my own call to conversion
so that I might become an example
of someone who has found great peace
in the arms of Christ.

May the joy I experience as a Catholic
be an invitation to those who are lost
to come home again
to the Church which we love.
Amen

Source: The Companions of St. Anthony, Conventional Franciscan
Friars, Saint Anthony of Padua province, Ellicott City, MD.

Suggested Personal "Act of Consecration to Sacred Heart of Jesus through the Immaculate Heart of Mary" (Shortened Version)

(From *Total Consecration according to Saint Louis Marie de Montfort,* Montfort Publications).

"I _____ *a faithless sinner, renew and ratify today in thy hands the vows of my Baptism; I renounce forever Satan, his pomps and works; and I give myself entirely to Jesus Christ, the Incarnate Wisdom, to carry my cross after Him all the days of my life, and to be more faithful to Him than I have ever been before.*

"In the presence of all the heavenly court, I choose thee this day for my Mother and mistress. I deliver and consecrate to thee, as thy slave, my body and soul, my goods, both interior and exterior, and even the value of all of my good actions, past, present, and future; leaving to thee the entire and full right of disposing of me and all that belongs to me, without exception, according to thy good pleasure, for the greater glory of God in time and in eternity."

Suggested Family Consecration to Jesus through Mary:

"Jesus, our most loving Redeemer, You came to enlighten the world with Your teaching and example. You willed to spend the greater part of Your life in humble obedience to Mary and Joseph in the poor home of Nazareth. In this way You sanctified that FAMILY which was to be an example for all CHRISTIAN FAMILIES.

"Graciously accept our(my) family which we(I) dedicate to You. Be pleased to protect, guard and keep it in holy fear,

in peace and in the harmony of Christian charity. By conforming ourselves to the Divine Model of Your Family, may we all attain to eternal happiness.

"Mary, Mother of Jesus and our Mother, by Your intercession, make this our(my) offering acceptable to Jesus and obtain for us graces and blessings.

"Saint Joseph, most holy guardian of Jesus and Mary, help us by your prayers in all our spiritual and temporal needs, so that we may praise Jesus our Divine Savior, together with Mary and you, for all eternity.

"Lord, we(I) pray that You visit our home and drive from it all snares of the enemy. Let Your Holy Angels dwell in it to preserve us in peace; and let Your Blessing be always upon us."

"Through the prayers of the Blessed Virgin Mary, we beg you to guard our family from all danger. As we humbly worship You with all our hearts, in Your mercy, graciously protect us from all the snares of the enemy and keep us in Your peace. We ask all this through Jesus Christ our Lord. AMEN."

Prayers of praise and thanksgiving to the Father for everything … He needs to be praised and thanked before we go off on our daily lives … Praise and thank your Guardian Angel asking him/her to be with you throughout the day.

Note: To consecrate means "To make holy and set aside for God's service." When you personally or as a family or for your family consecrate to Jesus through Mary, you are pledging and declaring that: "We are Yours and Yours we wish to be. This family (or yourself) will be at Your service. We (I) will return Your love for love. Your Heart(s) enthroned in our (my) home will be a reminder for us(me) and the model of our(my) love for one another."

St. Michael Prayer

"St. Michael the Archangel, defend me this day in the battle. Be my protection against the wickedness and snares of the devil (the evil one). May god rebuke him, I humbly pray, that Thou who are the Prince of the Heavenly Host, by the Divine power of God, cast into hell all the evil spirits who prowl about the world seeking the ruin of souls."

Prayer before starting to Pray

"Heavenly and Eternal Father, I now put the Precious Blood of Your dearly beloved Son, Jesus Christ, before my lips, my mind and my heart, before I begin to pray, that my prayers may be purified before they ascend to Your Heavenly Throne." *(author unknown).*

The Angel's Prayer from Fatima (in reparation)

O Most Holy Trinity, we believe in You, we adore You, we hope and trust in You, and we love You. We beg pardon of all those who do not believe in You, do not adore You, do not hope and trust in You, and do not love you, throughout the world. (This prayer can be said with the Rosary, after each decade, if one desires.)

Prayer from St. Margaret Mary

"O my Jesus and my Love, take all that I have and all that I am and possess me to the full extent of Thy good pleasure, since all I have is Thine without reserve. Transform me entirely into Thyself, so that I may no longer be able to separate myself from Thee for a single moment and that I may no longer act but by the impulse of Thy pure love."

Prayer to Holy Spirit

(Pray to the Holy Spirit, consecrating yourself to Him, and asking for His Gifts, Graces and Virtues.)

Suggestion: "Almighty and Eternal God, Who has vouchsafed to regenerate us by water and the Holy Spirit (Ghost), and has given us forgiveness of all sins, vouchsafe to send forth from heaven, upon us, Your sevenfold Spirit; the Spirit of Wisdom and Understanding, the Spirit of Counsel and Fortitude, the Spirit of Knowledge and Piety, and fill us with the Spirit of Holy Fear. Amen." (From Novena to Holy Spirit-Holy Ghost Fathers.)

Pray for Holy Souls in Purgatory
(taking a daily pilgrimage to Purgatory)

St. Margaret Mary wrote: *"In union with the divine Heart of Jesus make a short pilgrimage to Purgatory at night. Offer Him your activities of the day and ask Him to apply His merits to the suffering souls. At the same time implore them (the souls) to obtain for you the grace to live and die in the love and friendship of this Divine Heart. Fortunate will you be, if you succeed in obtaining deliverance for some of these imprisoned souls, for you will gain as many friends in heaven."*

Prayer for souls

"Eternal Father, we offer You the Passion, Death, and Resurrection of Jesus, and the sorrows of the Virgin Mary and St. Joseph, in payment for our sins, in prayer for the holy souls in Purgatory, for the needs of the Church, and for the conversion of sinners. Amen"(Missionaries of the Sacred Heart) **OR** *"Oh my God, in union with the merits of Jesus and Mary, I offer You for the souls in Purgatory, all my satisfactory works, as well as those which may be applied to me by others, during my life, and after my death. So as to be more agreeable to the Heart of Jesus and more helpful to the departed, I place them all in the hands of the merciful Virgin Mary. Amen."* **(St. Alphonse Liguori)**

Return Love to *"Love"*

Thoughts to Reflect on

How do you identify yourself as a Christian? How do people identify you as a Christian? Do you love all people, unconditionally? Do you harbor anger, resentments, judgments, criticize and condemn, even harm one of your brothers or sisters, or yourself?

May the Spirit of God enlighten and strengthen you to persevere in all of your resolutions and new found life in Him, that you may come to know the love of Christ that surpasses knowledge, so that you may be filled with all the fullness of God, at all times.

> **"Do everything through love and for love, making good use of the present moment. Do not be anxious about the future.**
>
> **"In order to make good use of time, we must love ardently and constantly; we must Surrender ourselves entirely to LOVE, leaving it to act for us. Be satisfied to adhere to it in everything, but always with profound humility."**
> (St. Margaret Mary)

Note: The teachings and lessons used for this meditation book, *Return Love to "LOVE,"* have been received in the form of locutions since 1988 for Harriet Hammons and 1992 for Carol Ameche. Each meditation is out of context and taken directly from the lessons and teachings found in the book and its supplement, "Do Whatever Love Requires." If you wish to delve more fully into one or more of the teaching meditations given for each day, we suggest you refer to the original books for the comprehensive teaching or lesson.